The Alchemy of Fear

The Alchemy of Fear

*How to Break the Corporate Trance and
Create Your Company's Successful Future*

Kay Gilley

Butterworth–Heinemann

Boston   Oxford   Johannesburg   Melbourne   New Delhi   Singapore

Recognizing the importance of preserving what has been written, Butterworth–Heinemann prints its books on acid-free paper whenever possible.

 Butterworth–Heinemann supports the efforts of American Forests and the Global ReLeaf program in its campaign for the betterment of trees, forests, and our environment.

Library of Congress Cataloging-in-Publication Data
Gilley, Kay 1949–
    The alchemy of fear : how to break the corporate trance and create your company's successful future / Kay Gilley.
        p.   cm.
    Includes bibliographical references.
    ISBN 0-7506-9909-4 (alk. paper)
    1. Job stress.   2. Job satisfaction.   3. Self-help techniques.   I. Title.
    HF5548.85.G53   1988
    158.7—DC21   97-25329
                                                                          CIP

British Library Cataloguing-in-Publication Data
A catalogue record for this book is available from the British Library.

The publisher offers special discounts on bulk orders of this book.
For information, please contact:

Manager of Special Sales
Butterworth–Heinemann
225 Wildwood Avenue
Woburn, MA 01801-2041
Tel: 617-928-2500
Fax: 617-928-2620

For information on all Butterworth–Heinemann business books available, contact our World Wide Web home page at: http://www.bh.com

10 9 8 7 6 5 4 3 2 1

Printed in the United States of America

*To all those who have brought fear into my life
and to all those who have helped me
transform my relationship to it*

Contents

Foreword

As I read *The Alchemy of Fear: How to Break the Corporate Trance and Create Your Company's Successful Future*, I realize that it is a resource I could have used many times in my career.

When I was building Watson Rice as Chairman/CEO what we most needed was an opportunity to accept rapid change without letting it tear the firm apart. We needed to build, grow, change, expand, contract, change marketing direction, refinance, and develop new services within short time frames. This rapid-growth environment caused much angst and stretched many of our partners beyond their capacity. Somehow we made the needed transitions, but life would have been much simpler if *The Alchemy of Fear* had been available then.

Had my partners at Watson Rice been able to cocreate a new direction when the federal government changed its contracting direction, my transition out could have been smoother.

This book does an excellent job of explaining the state of *not-knowing*. I have come to understand that it has been missing in many of our negotiations. As we grow to respect it and honor it as a place of collective learning and creation, we will be able to build a better world.

When we were in Brussels negotiating changes to the General Agreement on Tariffs and Trade (GATT), which resulted in the formation of the World Trade Organization (WTO), we needed to join minds and hearts in the pursuit of a purpose higher than national sovereignty or protecting ineffective national industries. Rapid changes in the global economy had caused many national governments and groups to fall back into a protectionist posture—just the opposite of what was needed at the time. At times staying in the state of not-knowing, which this book helps us understand and embrace, would have allowed the negotiators to realize common objectives and find solutions that would have brought higher rewards for all parties.

Had the United States negotiating team for GATT been able to hold the state of not-knowing long enough in dealing with the confrontation regarding European farm subsidies, global trade policies could be more open and inclusive today.

When the African National Congress (ANC) elected newly freed Nelson Mandela to lead them, he looked to the Association of Black Accountants of South Africa (ABASA) for business leadership and help in forming economic policy. ABASA's leaders needed a way to rise above personal and group insecurities to join with experienced leaders from North America and Europe in forging new alliances and setting new directions. I had the opportunity to work with them, and I used spiritual and intuitive sources to provide a context for the personal and group stretch that was required for ABASA to work with the new South African government. Some of these accountants are now senior advisors, some in cabinet or subcabinet posts, and many have made major contributions to the new South Africa.

Had ABASA been comfortable cocreating from a position of not-knowing during the change of South Africa's government and resulting economic shifts, South Africa's economy could be stronger today.

Transforming fear is vital to survival and success in today's world. The power we gain from being present in a continued state of not-knowing will allow us to tap intuitive powers and draw on rich sources of information in our subconscious—creating better leaders, institutions, decisions, and actions. It will focus and empower leaders of fast-growing companies or anyone living in an environment of constant change.

This book is quite specific in illustrating how to use existing skills, fears, and circumstances to lift the understanding and performance of an individual, business, or institution. Kay Gilley's knowledge and experiences can move your company from a high-risk/high-growth venture to a dynamic, creative, and effective one. She is also consulting with executives who are exploring spirituality in the workplace and working to strengthen business or personal relationships. These are areas where the skills uncovered in this book can be transforming.

Many executives of high-growth companies are like Deacon Willie, my imaginary friend and traveling companion, who was crawling under a street lamp as though looking for something one evening. When I came up and asked him what he was doing, he replied, "Looking for my keys." So I got on my knees and joined him in the search. After a while I asked, "Willie, just where did you drop your keys?" "Over by my car," he replied. "Then why are you looking under this street lamp?" "The light is better over here," he replied. *The Alchemy of Fear* provides portable lights to shine on lost keys.

THOMAS S. WATSON, JR.,
retired chairman/CEO, Watson Rice,
author, *Connecting People*

Acknowledgments

Dozens of people helped make this project possible. I am grateful to those who helped me when the book was being born, by either participating in electronic brainstorming or sharing their ideas about workplace fear. Thanks to my many clients who have willingly worked with their fears and by so doing helped me better understand how we transform our relationship to fear in the workplace. And, I am forever indebted to those who have supported me in transforming my own relationship to fear.

My thanks to Sheryl Fullerton, Karen Speerstra, and Heidi Banks for continuing to believe in me and for being such wonderful people with whom to work.

Special appreciation goes to Lynn Bonner, Amy Winkelman, Dave Peck, and Jim Hargreaves, who read the manuscript and helped me develop my own ideas more completely with their feedback and who did so with lightning speed to keep me moving toward my own deadline.

Finally, my deepest gratitude to Roger Powell, who not only was a reader but helped me come to a much deeper understanding of my own relationship with fear, assisted me in finding more effective ways of communicating it to others, and supported me throughout the writing process.

Author's Note

This book presents what are likely to be totally new concepts to many people. It makes a case for our need to transform our relationship to our emotions in our workplaces. We have suppressed our emotions and, by so doing, have filled our workplaces with zombies moving through the day in trances. We have robbed ourselves and our workplaces of energy, enthusiasm, joy, and creativity. We have robbed them of information critical to making decisions in this time of constant change and growing chaos.

You will find stories and observations from over 30 years in workplaces, mostly as an employee or manager but more recently as a consultant, as well as some ideas about what we must do to develop a healthier relationship to our emotions. Where possible, I have provided examples of how I have been involved in teaching people to work with their emotions.

Critical to building an environment in which emotional competence can develop and love can flourish is knowing that there are no prescriptions. This book is intended to give readers ideas that will stimulate dialogue and individual or group processes aimed at exploring what these ideas mean to each person, in each unique environment. Emotional competence cannot and should not be treated as the latest Management-of-the-Month Club trend to be installed or implemented by a team of consultants. What is most important is that developing emotional competence is a gradual process of building awareness and consciousness, of choosing to be awake in our work instead of asleep at the wheel.

This book will be most beneficial, then, if it is allowed to stimulate thinking, reflection and dialogue about what these ideas mean to each person. Those who rush through it looking for the "bottom line" will miss the point.

There is a growing movement internationally to begin building workplaces that nurture the human spirit. I am a strong advocate of this need. At the same time, I am as concerned as anyone about spirit being "implemented" in our workplaces. So it is the same with emotional competence and learning to accept and use our emotions at work. Both are deeply personal and make people quite vulnerable. They cannot be adopted and implemented like statistical process controls or TQM or the latest management program. We can successfully bring spirit and emotional competence to our workplaces only by learning to live them and build an environment in which they may bubble forth naturally.

Our emotions are the door to spirit. We have been trying to get spirit and all that it brings without even paying lip service to our emotions. It won't work. It is my hope that *The Alchemy of Fear* will provide a key to opening that important door.

Recovering from Organizational Brain Damage

"Most people think courage is the absence of fear. The absence of fear is not courage; the absence of fear is some kind of brain damage."

... M. SCOTT PECK, *Further Along the Road Less Traveled*[1]

Alchemy—the word conjures up a variety of notions, depending on one's interests and experiences. The commonality among all of the understandings of *alchemy* is that it is a magical process that changes something of little value into something of great value.

The concept of alchemy was popularized in medieval times in two different but parallel contexts. Their common roots lay in the understanding of alchemy as an "apparently magical power or transmutation process."[2] Again, both constructs incorporate changing something that was undesirable or of little value into something desirable and valuable.

The first concept was a philosophy of chemistry "that had as its asserted aims the transmutation of base metals into gold."[3] Most commonly, practitioners of this magical process had as their objective chemically converting lead into gold.

The second concept of alchemy emerged as an important part of the traditions of both Christian and Jewish medieval mystics (whose beliefs were based on their personal experience of God) of self-development and spiritual growth. They believed that a process, which paralleled that of changing base metals into gold, occurred as an individual evolved spiritually. Typically, as a person worked to grow spiritually, he or she would evolve from what has been called *prima materia*, or the raw material we are given when we start life, into a higher order of being that is much more godlike, powerful, and even magical in nature.

The mystics believed that full realization of our spiritual potential is similar to a second birth because we become a new person in the process. Our lives after the process of spiritual alchemy are rich with promise and possibility that didn't exist in us prior to the development process.

Psychologist C. G. Jung was intrigued with this concept of spiritual alchemy because it corresponded closely to his seminal study of human psychological development. He called the process *individuation* and described it as a process of becoming whole. During individuation, his work indicated, we evolve from individuals of limited potential and possibility to ones with limitless potential. Jung used *archetypes*, or metaphorical descriptions, to describe the various stages or characteristics of this process of becoming more whole.

In the earlier stages of individuation, Jungians use the Orphan archetype to describe our feeling of being alone and our need to take responsibility for our lives on our own. When we are living the Orphan archetype, we learn important lessons of self-reliance and independence, which allow us to take care of ourselves physically in the world. This also can be a frightening stage because it is characterized by a feeling of isolation, disconnectedness, and even desperation, experienced because we have to take on life without the nurturing support of spiritual dimensions.

When we have "individuated," as Jung described those who have evolved through their psychological development, Jungians use the archetype of the Magician. The Magician feels supported and nurtured by God, the Universe, God within, or another supporting divine presence. Even though the Magician may be physically alone, he or she always feels supported by the realm of the divine. The Magician therefore can transform circumstances that otherwise might be described as negative into openings for new possibilities.

Alchemy in the psychological sense is a process whereby we transform ourselves through many stages into Magicians who live as more whole and harmonious beings.

What Does Alchemy Have to Do with My Workplace?

What does all of this have to do with fear and building more effective organizations in the 21st century? After 30 years of working both in and with organizations, I have come to believe that much of what occurs in our organizations is driven by fear. The globalization of the economy and the rapid and ever-changing development of technology have combined to produce work environments that are intensely competitive, unpredictable, and often chaotic. Faced with the almost daily demand to learn new ways of working, fear, usually unacknowledged, has created a level of stress in most of us that can be physically exhausting at best and life-threatening at worst.

The connection between alchemy and fear is that our unnamed personal and collective fears hold the potential for personal and organizational alchemy unlike any most of us have experienced. The base nature of denied fears leads us to ineffective action. We make futile attempts to control the uncontrollable. We store these fears in our bodies, and they make us physically sick. When we are able to engage a transmutation process, beginning with acknowledging and naming our fears, we are able to experience the magic of alchemy. Our fears can be gifts. Rather than stopping us from acting or learning new ways of living and working, they can catalyze a process that will tell us what we need to consider or learn. They can help us master new ways of working. Our fears hold vast amounts of information when we are willing and able to draw them from the subconscious into conscious, rational processes of work. When we grow to value and utilize our fears, they become "golden" to us.

In *Leading from the Heart*,[4] I said that, to be effective in this new world, we must focus on our "being" and not our "doing." Everything I've learned since then has reinforced this perspective. I said the being was a being of courage that allowed us to be constantly and consciously aware of our fears without letting our fears consume us.

I have been studying people for many years. I believe that, even in much less chaotic times, more than 90 percent of what occurs in our workplaces is motivated by fear. In fact, I would guess that nearly 90 percent of what occurs in our *lives* is motivated by fear. Although unnamed, unacknowledged, and even denied, fear drives our organizations, fear has become the four-letter "F-word" that no one wants to say or acknowledge. In many organizations, talking about one's fears is tantamount to professing incompetence. Denial is rampant. People have learned to use words in ways that let them trick themselves into believing they aren't afraid, while they are actually saying they are. They usually come up with sound rational reasons and processes, designed to restrict the free flow of information, which themselves grew from fear.

One way I've come to understand how prevalent fear is results from the responses I get when I ask individuals or groups what they want. They are most likely to respond by telling what they don't want, which is what they fear. So, I might ask, "What do you want from this new initiative? How will we know whether it is a success or not?"

Almost without fail, they will begin by telling me, "We don't want what happened in the XYZ project," or "We don't want what happened to Acme Co.," or "We don't want to lose control." What they are actually saying is, "We are afraid that what happened in the XYZ project will happen again," or "We are afraid that what happened to the Acme Co. will happen to us," or "We are afraid we will lose control." Yet, when I follow up by clarifying that they are afraid of these things, they will insist that they aren't afraid!

Learning to consciously acknowledge and accept these fears and "be with them" is critical in our workplaces. I can think of no other aspect of our work about which we would allow the level of denial and avoidance that we do with fear. We not only allow the denial, we encourage it. Similar to what Scott Peck has said about us personally, the belief that workplace fears don't exist can be attributed only to some sort of brain damage. Most of our organizations are run with such a level of denial that it is as if we were organizationally brain damaged. Our fears keep us locked in self-censorship, censorship of those around us, and intimidation, afraid to say what needs to be said.

One organization in which I worked had experienced similar operational effectiveness problems for 20 years, but the people who worked there were afraid of what they might find if they really started to look at themselves. When I first started working with them, the first thing they wanted to do was have an agenda and know that they weren't going to be "taking on something that was 'inappropriate'." Then, they quickly classified anything that might get to the root of their problems as "inappropriate." It took eight days of meetings over four months before they were willing to let go of agenda control and begin speaking from their hearts. When they did, change began.

This group had been forced by a changing market environment to do business differently, or I am convinced that they still would not have confronted their interactional issues, which were causing widespread ineffectiveness. Change becomes the engine of fear. As change speeds up, the engine produces more and more fear. The only way to keep change from driving an organization out of control is to start talking about what the engine is.

In recent years, this organization had been faced with serious competition for the first time. After several years of struggling for survival, it felt understaffed and undercapitalized for daily operations, and those who worked there thought they needed significantly more research and development money to compete. Thin profit margins prevented increasing prices, and several years of cutting expenses left the organization with few sources to prune dollars. A climate of fear reigned over the whole company. All the members of the organization had their backs to the wall while looking for ways to cut expenses in another department.

Only when they were willing to start talking about what they feared, including the demise of the company and the need for each of them to learn new ways to work, did they begin to discover ways to both improve their effectiveness without spending more money and cut costs without slashing positions. They discovered duplicated efforts. They discovered certain activities were being performed that no one needed. They discovered that, if they used their current technology to its capacity, much work could be eliminated. They freed countless hours that could be dedicated to projects that would improve their competitive advantage but had been shelved because of lack of budget resources to finance them.

In our work worlds, change is occurring so rapidly that we cannot know what will be the most effective response years, months, weeks, and sometimes even days in advance. We must avail ourselves of the full range of possibilities. We must hold ourselves in a place of "not-knowing," making a conscious choice to be flexible, open, curious, and inquiring, embracing that we do not and cannot know what the most effective action will be.

That place of not-knowing is both frightening and counterintuitive for most of us. Being in not-knowing means we choose to give up control. Letting go of control is incredibly difficult for most of us because we are *afraid* of the unknown. How we deal with fear largely will determine how we effectively cope in a world of continuous change so that we remain healthy personally and work in a way that benefits the long-term health of the organization. It will determine how we see the world. Will we see it like the Magician would, as a friendly place with many possibilities? Or will we see it as a frightened Orphan would see it, as a threatening place in which we must adopt a personal and organizational modus operandi of defensiveness and protectionism, because at best we see limited possibilities.

Our worldview, or what has been called our *paradigm*, defines our limitations. If our worldview is one of the Magician with many possibilities, we will see few limitations. Talking about our fears then is a logical, rational thing to do. If our worldview is one of the Orphan from which we are perpetually threatened, all we will see are limitations. Overwhelmed by the prospect of simply surviving, we will want to deny our fears, hoping that if we don't talk about them, they will go away.

Our organizations have asked us to compartmentalize ourselves and leave our emotions at home. Our culture, in general, has been ill at ease with the concept of whole individuals who come with emotions as standard and essential equipment. As a culture, it is time that we began to consciously heal ourselves.

"I'm already overburdened. I work more than ever. It's more stressful. I'm torn between work and family. How can you ask me to take more time to heal ourselves?"

We have exhausted ourselves fighting to keep fear and all of our emotions at bay. Because we are so tired is exactly why we should be doing it.

We spend almost half of our waking lives at work. Whatever is happening at work without fail will affect the rest of our lives as well as our physical health. Both because of the inevitable impact on us personally and because the effectiveness of our workplaces has been so significantly influenced by our emotional incompetence, our organizations seem to be ripe for championing a process of emotional reintegration. Our workplaces should be paths of personal growth. We can become alchemists who transform our emotional lead into gold. We have the potential to turn dreaded, denied, unacknowledged fear into a dynamic force for good in our organizations and for the growth of the people in them.

A new worldview of our organizations is in order. If we are to recover from our organizational brain damage, we need a worldview of oneness, from which we see a new role, with a new set of expectations, that redefines what we talk about and do at work—one that embraces the whole human beings that make up the organization.

I will fully acknowledge that this is not the stuff of traditional business schools. It is hard work personally, and it is hard to integrate into days that already appear to be too full. But there is an organizational and personal imperative: the old way is not working. The price has been too high, and yet we have voluntarily continued to pay it in lost revenue, increased expenses, loss of human capital, ineffective decisions, and lack of joy in our work.

To keep fear buried, we have silently and unconsciously agreed to keep "down" all of our emotional reactions, the good as well as the bad. The result is that, at a time when creativity, capability, courage, and joy are desperately needed in our organizations, they are unavailable to us. It is time for our workplaces to be alive, to become stimulating, exciting places in which to spend our time, to be places to which we look forward to going and in which we are eagerly growing. Acknowledging and coming to peace with our personal workplace fears, as well as our organizational ones, will go a long way toward bringing emotional competence into our lives.

Although "empowerment" has been talked about in our workplaces for years, it rarely has been actualized. A person who brings his or her fears to consciousness and discovers how to move toward them begins to experience how he or she can create new and more satisfying outcomes and relationships. In actuality, the key to the creation of the circumstances of our lives has been uncovered, bringing real meaning and life to "empowerment" and making a case for personal growth of the people in it as the new work of the organization. The dynamic organization of the future can prosper only as its people grow.

It is time to bring workplace fear out of the closet and offer ideas about how we can transform our relationship with fear from one of denial, fight, flight, and repression to one in which fear is openly understood, accepted, respected, and even embraced as a gift, a teacher, and a friend. When we learn to transform fear from a negative to be avoided or overcome into a positive quality to be honored and valued, we will be able to use it for both personal and organizational learning. When we finally are able to recognize and talk about our fears, we will dramatically improve the quality of our decisions and our workplace relationships, as well as our lives in general. When we stop denying our fears and begin naming them, we open ourselves and our workplaces to peace, passion, and possibility unlike any we have known.

I also hope that the journey toward embracing fear will stimulate readers to begin to value what I call *emotional competence*. Emotional competence is a healthy, mature relationship with our own emotions and the emotions of others. Only in the last 75 years have organizations begun to accept the importance of physical health in the workplace, evidenced as employers began routinely sponsoring first medical and later dental and vision insurance. Workplace safety programs and even health and wellness programs are now common. Organizations must understand that emotional health and competence are just as essential for organizational well-being as physical health has become.

My goal is to give readers a handbook for transforming their relationship with fear in their work activities by presenting ideas about how fears can be brought forth and used for learning. This process will lead to an understanding of how we honor the emotion without the emotionality. When we are able to do this, we will experience a new level of organizational effectiveness. People truly will be empowered to work together to create the circumstances of their work lives and organizational outcomes.

Finally, this book will introduce what it means to be working together in continual cocreation, the 21st century way of doing work. It will describe how essential both emotional competence and a perspective of the workplace as a place of wholeness are to that process.

It is time to learn the magic of alchemy that can come to our organizations when we learn to accept and effectively use our emotions, including fear. This book will break new ground and stimulate dialogue about how we can and must work together differently to come to life organizationally and individually. When individuals and groups develop the courage to talk about what they fear, they inevitably discover new ways of approaching challenges. Simultaneously, they develop a commitment to a conscious course of action that often generates an excitement and enthusiasm which comes from feeling confident that they are on the right track.

Transforming the Fear

- Alchemy is a magical process that changes something of little value into something of great value. In spiritual alchemy, we evolve from the "raw material" we are at the start of life into a higher order of being that is more godlike, powerful, and magical in nature. In psychological alchemy, we evolve from Orphans, feeling alone and with few possibilities, into Magicians, who, supported by the divine, see themselves as full of potential and life as full of possibility.
- The connection between alchemy and fear is that our unnamed personal and collective fears hold the potential for a similar alchemical process that opens new opportunities and possibilities.
- The world is changing so rapidly that we must learn to hold ourselves in a place of "not-knowing," making a conscious

choice to be flexible, open, curious, and inquiring, embracing that we do not and cannot know what the most effective action will be.

- Our organizations have asked us to compartmentalize ourselves and leave our emotions at home. To keep fear buried, we have silently agreed to keep down all of our emotions, leaving our organizations desperately needing creativity, capability, courage, and joy.
- The dynamic organization of the future can prosper only as its people grow. The new work of the organization, then, must be the personal growth of the people in it.

2

Facing Our Fears

"Courage is the capacity to go ahead in spite of the fear,
or in spite of the pain. When you do that, you will find
that overcoming that fear will not only make you stronger
but will be a big step forward toward maturity."
. . . M. SCOTT PECK, Further Along the Road Less Traveled[1]

Just as I was starting work on this book, I had the most incredible opportunity to learn more about the nature of fear in a chaotic world. I was awakened at 2 a.m. to discover I was experiencing my first hurricane. As I looked out the fiercely shaking sliding glass doors, I observed what can be described only as complete chaos. A 10-foot-high hedge was being blown almost flat to the ground, and it appeared to be raining sideways. The howl was deafening. The walls were shaking so hard a large heavy painting was pulled off the wall, hooks and all. By the next morning, thousands of trees had been uprooted, frequently damaging or destroying homes as they fell.

This is how it is in organizations now—complete chaos. Hardly anything is behaving the way we expect it to. As the hurricane roared, I suddenly became aware of the steady chirping of the crickets, as if nothing unusual were occurring. I was reminded that order always is implicit in chaos—and the potential for chaos always exists in order. Earlier the day before, when the sun was shining, it had been just as hard to imagine that a few hours later I would be in the middle of a devastating hurricane.

Never before in human history have people been asked to change as often and as quickly. We now must integrate new information, new technology, and rapidly evolving market conditions and expectations. Many of us find ourselves feeling emotionally, psychologically, and spiritually, if not physically and intellectually, whipped about by the daily forces in our work worlds. We constantly face the intensity of a figurative hurricane. Change always has been inevitable, but taxpayers, government agencies, business owners, customers, suppliers, special-interest groups, and countless others, intent on creating what their own stakes demand, leave us feeling as if we have been pulled about, twisted, and torn, with a total lack of control. The order is always there, but often it feels as though the world is changing too quickly for us to take time to notice where the order remains.

At the same time, prognosticators predict that soon the change will become even more fluid, requiring us to adapt even more quickly to different roles in almost every facet of our lives in the new millennium. Futurists in every field are projecting a new world in the near future. There will be a shift in how we look at and do almost everything, and the changes are occurring at breakneck speed (see box).

Clearly, a shift is taking place in how we will successfully relate in all aspects of our lives. The changes are occurring at such breakneck speed, practically as fast as they are being predicted, that we are left with little or no time to prepare. Although some of us are just beginning to be comfortable with concepts like self-directed work teams and many more of us are beginning to adjust to integrating more teamwork into what we do, we are being told this is not enough. We must forsake these constructs and become comfortable with even more fluid structures, such as self-organizing systems.

Projected Futures in Different Fields

Field	Perspective	Demand
Organizational forms	"We are one and choose to cocreate"	A communitarian structure in the Fourth Wave[2]
Health, healing, medicine	"An encounter with one's own wholeness"	"Shift away from fragmentation and isolation toward wholeness and connectedness"[3]
Global environment	Planetary health	We cannot win if the Earth loses. Concern by companies and individuals.

Yet even with the variety of predictions of change, common themes are seen in every arena: wholeness, more openness and sharing, more mutual and self-acceptance, working together in flexible, fluid structures in continual cocreation. Some of us, at least conceptually, embrace these changes. Few of us are prepared personally to make the changes necessary to function healthfully and effectively in this new world. To do so, we are required to give up control, having the answer, and even traditional goal-setting and planning activities. We must each embrace chaos and not-knowing and search for new ways to measure success.

Frankly, when we are being honest, most of us are frightened to death by the prospect.

Most corporate executives would not openly admit to being afraid, but scratch beneath the surface of any action they take, any decision they make, or any discussion they have, and one or many fears usually are present. What's not said is even more telling of fear's presence than what is said. More truth emerges in the unofficial meeting in the bathroom, the corridor, or the parking lot after the meeting than in the meeting itself. We're afraid to speak up and share our truths. We're afraid to say what everyone around us knows but is afraid to say. We're afraid to hear anything that contradicts our fictional beliefs of how things really are. We're afraid to really explore our espoused beliefs of how things are in order to discover if there is any reality to them at all.

Even though an environment of truth is essential in our 21st century organizations, Maynard and Mehrtens suggest that it is fear that prevents this atmosphere of truth from prevailing:

> People see the lies and abuses, the destruction of those among them who dare to be bold, iconoclastic, creative. They sense the lack of trust, the fear that is palpable in the corridors and the offices. They manifest the pathology of "group think" in meetings, where silence greets the manager's call for problems or differing viewpoints. Employees in corporate America today live in fear of being seen as wrong, of making a mistake, of being fired, busted, or neutralized. Those with the temerity to speak truth to power usually suffer for it, and the net result of all this is to leave the corporation stuck in the morass of the 'party line,' paralyzed by fear and deceit. . . . The reporting or discussion of bad news is avoided . . . because people live in fear of hurting others or of being hurt themselves. (Maynard and Mehrtens, *The Fourth Wave*[4])

Fear is an underlying cause of several organizational learning disabilities described by Peter Senge in his long-standing best seller *The Fifth Discipline*:[5]

- "The Enemy Is Out There" describes the behavior that results when we are afraid to look at our own role in creating problems and take responsibility for ourselves, rather than looking for others to blame.
- "The Illusion of Taking Charge" occurs when "we simply become more aggressive fighting the 'enemy out there'. . . . True proactiveness comes from seeing how we contribute to our own problems," something most of us are afraid to do.

- "The Myth of the Management Team" occurs because people really are concerned about looking bad personally. They want to protect their own interests, but they don't want to be seen as someone who isn't a "team player."

Senge describes how many of us find ourselves living the myth:

> School trains us to never admit that we do not know the answer, and most corporations reinforce that lesson by rewarding the people who excel in advocating their views, not inquiring into complex issues. . . . Even if we are uncertain or ignorant, we learn to protect ourselves from the pain of appearing uncertain or ignorant. That very process blocks out any new understandings which might threaten us. The consequence is what Argyris calls "skilled incompetence"— teams full of people who are incredibly proficient at keeping themselves from learning. (Senge, *The Fifth Discipline*[6])

We have been "incredibly proficient at keeping [our]selves from learning." We are afraid we might look bad before our peers and bosses. We are afraid of *what* we might learn, afraid of changes that we might have to make based on what we learn. We are afraid to find out our whole world is based on the illusion that any of us can really know how things are.

Although Senge doesn't say so, perhaps our biggest organizational learning disability is our inability or unwillingness, or both, to recognize our fears and the destructive roles they lead us to play, again and again and again. Despite many signs everywhere that fear drives our organizations, denial is rampant. Giving voice to fear has been tantamount to admitting incompetence, disloyalty, a career-limiting move, or committing organizational suicide.

Why Does It Matter?

When fears are denied, those making decisions, whether individually or collectively, inevitably will work in a time dimension other than the present. They will be fearful about what has happened (or what almost happened to them) in the past or what happened to someone else in the past. This causes them to do one of two things:

- They will focus on avoiding, in the future, what happened, almost happened, or might have happened in the past.
- They will push for producing predictable results at the expense of creativity, inventiveness, and possibility.

Either way, all the while, they miss the present. Why is missing the present so significant? Because it is the only time in which they can make any change that actually would prevent the occurrence of the unacceptable outcomes they wanted to avoid. It also is the only time dimension in which creativity can occur.

How can we have a different relationship with fear, one in which we aren't controlled by it? The answer is to choose the only rational relationship to fear—one that names the fears in present time and develops a strategy for action in the present. The action must be conscious, capable, creative, and courageous. But before we can transform our relationship to fear we must understand it and know how it functions in our lives and in our workplaces.

What Is Fear?

Fear is the most primitive of emotions. It is housed in what is called the *limbic system*, specifically the amygdala. This part of the brain relates to our most basic survival mechanisms. Because it controls our very survival, the amygdala never forgets; it just keeps adding data—data to support its most core beliefs. Because fear is so primitive and about survival, it is not logical, thoughtful, or in any way intellectual. The thinking part of our brain developed much later.

Daniel Goleman, who has spent years researching what he calls our "emotional intelligence," explains, "The thinking brain literally grew out of the emotional brain, making it possible for the emotional brain to hijack the thinking brain during bursts of rage, fear or other emotional alarms."[7]

My functional definition of fear includes two components:

- We are powerless to change something that we believe will occur.
- Somehow we are threatened by the projected inevitable outcome.

Because fear developed at a time in our evolution when a threat meant life-and-death survival, on a reactive level it is not adept at recognizing the differences between a real life-and-death threat and a threat to our ego or status quo. It lacks the rational ability to assess the true nature of the threat before it reacts.

Early on, the primitive part of the brain developed a set of ways of surviving when it thought we were powerless to change an outcome. These work automatically when we are threatened in any way. The fear reaction that we experience may or may not be on a conscious level. In more primitive times, the automatic response may have looked like crouching, or tensing our muscles in preparation to fight. Or, it may have looked like dropping our load and running like crazy to get away from the threat. Neither of these reactions is acceptable in a modern conference room; they would truly threaten our workplace survival. Our incredibly adaptable fear mechanism has produced more socially acceptable behavioral responses for our era. The reaction to shift into an analytical mode and look for problems is one such common automatic response.

If someone stands facing us with a loaded pistol, we will probably be conscious of a racing heartbeat, fast, shallow breathing, increased perspiration, and a surge of adrenaline. If a proposal is made in a meeting to push decision making to lower levels, potentially causing us to lose control as we have known it, we may be less aware of the physiological reaction, as our analytical side reacts by presenting possible problems that would have to be planned for. We may not be aware of it, but fear was there just the same.

Originally, our bodily reaction was designed to prepare us physically for fight or flight, either taking on our threat physically or getting the heck out of there. All of our responses prepared us to fight for our survival or escape from the threat. The adrenaline that is released allows us to perform feats of heroic proportion for a short window of time. (This is evidenced by periodic news reports of a mother lifting a car to rescue her child and similar stories.) This survival mechanism happens automatically.

While these automatic physical and mental changes are happening, our brain also is producing an automatic behavioral reaction, a set of actions, language, and body language that we perform *without thinking* when we perceive a threat. I call these *trances*.

When we were duking it out in the jungles or hoofing it out of the forest, the physiological changes stimulated by the threat produce a behavioral survival trance. We use that extra heart action and adrenaline to physically react to the threat. Our modern-day survival trances do just the opposite. They stifle all evidence of fear and project an illusion of confidence, competence, and control, all the while storing the stress in our bodies. An accumulation of stored fear reactions and trance responses leaves us sleepwalking through life, rarely in present time and space. Many of us numb our pain with alcohol, drugs, work, food, and a host of process addictions. The result is a populace riddled with stress-related or stress-generated health and addiction problems and chronic depression.

We weave our fear-driven behaviors together in habit systems to create our trances. Many of our trances are almost as old as we are. They become automatic responses, our way of operating on some kind of human automatic pilot. This, in turn, prevents us from thinking about what we are doing at this moment and realizing that we are making choices hundreds of times during the day. Our workplace trances include a host of perfectly rational sounding excuses that keep us from thinking about what we are doing in the present time:

- "It's not on the agenda."
- "We don't have time to talk about that."
- "We don't have the money to do that."
- "It would violate our policy."
- "It isn't in the budget this year."

These and many like them are automatic trance responses that rarely, if ever, get challenged but keep us from looking at the real issues of the organization or questioning our priorities. Our trances guide us through unconscious choices—choices to continue the masquerade that has led us to believe conditions cannot be changed.

As we enter new situations and relationships, we reemerge into consciousness just long enough to figure out which of our previously programmed trances can be modified most appropriately to work in this situation, subconsciously make the adjustments, and then relax back into automatic pilot. Over time, our autopilot carries us on what would appear to be a painless ride through life.

At one time in my consulting practice, I began the work with extensive interviews of employees. Frequently, the employer's representative would try to steer me away from newcomers, thinking and often expressing that the individual had not been with the company long enough to have anything to contribute. This was *exactly* the person I wanted to interview. The newcomer was in the process of learning what the company's trances were. If I could talk with these newcomers before they had fallen into the same trances, I could learn a lot about what caused the company's dysfunctions.

When a newcomer asks questions about how or why things are done or offers suggestions, he or she learns a lot about the company's trances. It is the natural tendency to want to figure out which of our existing trances work in the new place of em-

Trance response	What the employee learns
"That's not the way we do it."	"They're not open to new ideas." "Don't try anything new."
"Joe did it once and really got in trouble."	"People get in trouble for trying new things."
"That's not our policy."	"Know the rules and follow them. No room for creativity here."

ployment, so we listen, integrate the answers into our existing trance bank, and then shift back to autopilot (see box).

In my work, I often hear stories from people who saw problems when they joined a new organization. Oftentimes, they asked questions or made suggestions about improving things, and more often than not, they got a response that amounted to, "Nothing is going to change here." In no time at all, their old trance that told them "keep your mouth shut and just blend in" clicked in, and they shifted into an autopilot mode that supported the way things had always been done.

At the same time, that individual may have been brought into the company expressly because "new blood" was needed. When new ideas were presented, however, instead of embracing and exploring them, incumbents go into an "explanation" trance that describes why the new ideas won't work. This response happens so automatically that virtually no one ever thinks about what is occurring. I have heard many work teams described how this process has transpired over and over again, despite their espoused objective to bring in new thinking and totally without their awareness that it is happening.

If we truly want new thinking and creative approaches at work, we want to engage the newcomer in a dialogue that demonstrates that the company is open to change. But to do this, we have to be awake. We can't fall back on our trances. We have to think, listen, and ask questions. Instead of falling into a trance that says, "That wouldn't work here," we have to engage the person with questions like, "How would it work?" "What would be required to make the change?" "What benefits would we receive from the new approach that we don't have now?" "What would be potential problems?" "How would we integrate it into related systems?" These questions tell the newcomer that the person is present, listening, and interested. They also tell the newcomer that, if we have ideas, we should give them serious thought, and that we expect coworkers to help us develop ideas.

Our fear-induced trances allow us to cope with the situation literally "without thinking." They were designed to help us survive. The problem is that they are triggered in a whole range of situations that rarely have anything to do with survival.

In dealing with "new blood" in an organization, new ideas may be a threat to the status quo, which may mean that we need to learn new ways of working together. This, in turn, may offer the possibility of failure. It is a bit of a stretch to the thinking parts of our brains that, because we are unable to learn new work habits, we are going to die. Not so for the amygdala, which is where we are operating. The primitive part of the brain does an instantaneous scenario that looks like, "I might have to learn something new. I might fail. I might get fired. I might not get another job. I might starve to death." Click. Autopilot response: "That wouldn't work here because. . . ." Not rational, but our fear responses aren't rational.

It is important at this point to remind you that most of this is happening *without thinking about it*, in a trance state. When I have had the opportunity to stop the trance and ask people about the process, the thinking part of their brain almost always gives them a different response. However, if we don't stop the trance, we fall into our primitive response mode, where change is impossible.

Fear in the Workplace

Our fight-or-flight survival trances are particularly troublesome in our workplaces. In addition to keeping most of the organization from being present most of the time, they distract us from more effective ways of working together—ways our primitive survival mechanism sees as a potential threat because we've never worked that way before and *we may not be able to survive.*

First, let's clarify what I mean by *organizational fears.* I divide them into subtle fears and not-so-subtle fears. When I talk about workplace fear, what comes to most people are the fears of the not-so-subtle type. In an era of downsizing, right-sizing, reengineering, and decentralization, when even companies like IBM, which have long exemplified job security, have experienced significant layoffs, there is a lot of fear about job security.

What is evolving is a new concept of security. We are moving from one of dependence on the organization to take care of us to one of interdependence, where we take care of ourselves *and* the organization and vice versa. But to effectively take care of either ourselves or the organization, we must have the confidence to know that our ideas are good, important and without sharing them, neither we nor the company will do well. We also must have enough self-confidence to know that, if the organization does not want our ideas, we will be valuable to other employers.

We are changing from an era in which a secure job in a large organization was the norm to one in which each of us is an entrepreneur, either within our companies or between organizations. Sometimes that means new employment, but often it means that we strike out on our own. In any case, this isn't an easy adjustment for many to make, and so a lot of fear relates to this shift.

Those who retain their jobs after a downsizing often suffer from "survivors' syndrome." They become guarded, fearing that, if they honestly and fully participate, anything they say or do "can and will be used against" them. The survivors, literally in a survival mode, largely are trapped in a trance that says they are dependent on the organization for their survival. They have not yet shifted to thinking about themselves as personal entrepreneurs. They believe that they cannot change anything because the primitive survival mechanism has them believing that if they don't have their current job, they won't live.

Thinking of oneself as a personal entrepreneur is a whole new worldview. It will take time, learning, and adaptation. Eventually, the thought of being dependent on an organization will seem archaic to us, but while we are learning how to play the role of personal entrepreneur, it is frightening. Our worldview defines our limitations. While we are in the old worldview, all we can see are frightening circumstances that threaten us. When we break into a new worldview—one rich with possibilities—we will wonder how we could have let ourselves be so limited. But we have to walk through our fear to get there.

With only one exception, every person that I know who has gone through the downsizing or other job termination has more pleasure, satisfaction, and potential in his or her new work than in the previous position. Some actually had been unhappy in the position for a long time and lacked the courage to make the move. The transition was hard for most all of them, but I am sure that none would return to the jobs that kept them locked in their fear-driven dependence. The one exception is a man who became frozen in his fear, certain that he would not survive. He hasn't found a job, and he is hardly surviving. But despite his miserable condition, he refuses to even entertain the idea that his fear might be contributing to his own circumstances.

The other type of not-so-subtle fear is management by intimidation. Perpetuated by insecure Machiavellians who must continuously boost their needy egos by failing to respect those for whom and with whom they work, they sustain themselves by constantly taking an extra pound of flesh from those who work for them. That may manifest in continuous threats, rejections, and controlling behaviors or in sexual or racial harassment. It is an ugly side of our organizations, and it is an ugly side of humanity. These managers often cycle many employees through their departments, divisions, or organizations. The only people that seem to stay are those that are prone to see themselves as victims who live locked in fear of moving into their own personal power. They create a classic and self-perpetuating dependent-codependent relationship.

Subtle fears are much more pervasive and damaging than the not-so-subtle ones. These not-so-subtle fears are superficial products of much deeper and more subtle fears. Subtle fears are harder to recognize and identify, and they almost invariably underlie the not-so-subtle fears. So, for instance, people may say they are afraid of being downsized out of a job, which is the not-so-subtle fear, but really are afraid of a threat to their physical survival, which is the subtle, underlying fear. Or the subtle fear may be that the job loss will begin the disintegration of the family unit, resulting in loss or change of important relationships.

One might think that we should attack the not-so-subtle fears first, to get down to the subtle ones. In fact, just the opposite is true. We should acknowledge and work with the subtle fears, to reclaim our power, ability, and confidence to address the not-so-subtle ones as well. The subtle fears are the fears that people deny they have and then use different words (uneasiness, confusion, uncomfortable, frustrated, irritated, etc.) to describe them. These are fears like fear of change, fear of loss of control, fear of accountability, fear of abandonment, fear of not being liked, fear of success, and fear of survival.

Fight or Flight at Work

The "fight" response may manifest itself at work as an adversarial relationship with a coworker, but I more often see it emerging as what might be termed *passive-aggressive* behavior—creating impediments in ways that don't look like that's what is being done. Usually without even knowing it intellectually, a person is afraid of an outcome associated with a particular course of action. For example, a new course of action may be similar to one with which an individual has negative associations. The primitive part of the brain responds with behaviors that either prevent the decision or, once a decision has been made, prevent implementation.

This kind of reactive behavior may occur at a number of different points in the process. I often see it as agenda control. The individual(s) try to keep an item off the agenda, or if it makes it to the agenda, then they see that it is a low priority and somehow always just manage to run out of time before it is considered. Other times, when it does come up, additional information will be needed, so the topic is tabled for a long time. Once a decision is made, this passive aggressive "fight" may surface as deadlines being delayed on projects because other activities demanded staff time or some other perfectly feasible-sounding excuse that prevents implementation of the decision.

Fight may also appear in the form of a champion for a cause. If the subject is one that cannot be avoided, then discussion often gets "packaged" under the guise of "doing your homework" and is presented in a fashion in which the person (or people) who is afraid of it can "push it through" without opening up a serious dialogue. This set of behaviors can be motivated by a number of different fear positions. It may be that a particular initiative appears inevitable and the champion wants to control *how* it will happen. The champion pushes for a course that ensures he or she will be able to "survive" and look good. It may be used to distract the decision makers from an alternative course of action that somehow is personally threatening to the champion. Perhaps, the champion is on shaky ground and doesn't want to open his or her ideas to scrutiny. By putting forth a thorough analysis and assessment with recommendations, others are distracted from alternative approaches, or if they have other thoughts, the confidence with which the ideas were presented can cause dissenters to be afraid to share a different view.

One manager with whom I have worked quite a bit was famous for championing. He would put a package together and then do a hard sell to get the rest of the management team to adopt his idea without serious dialogue. More than once, his schemes became nightmares, but he was a good salesman. While I was working with the team, he tried his fight trance, but the team chose to involve me so they could use the deliberations for group learning. We spent time coming to understand the concerns that needed to be addressed and learning how to best accomplish this. It did not take long for the group to discover that the package the manager had contrived would not have even met basic needs. The group collectively built what eventually was a much better solution. But, as they did, this manager became visibly uncomfortable and critical. What they were designing was pushing him far out of his comfort zone. It required him to share power, involve others, and learn new behaviors. Although I was not involved in many meetings in which this "champion" sold his fellow managers a package, it is a fairly safe bet that he pushed initiatives with which he was comfortable because he was afraid of trying new things and afraid of failure.

The "flight" response often occurs in the same conference room as championing. It is what Senge called *the myth of the management team*. Decision makers appear to be in agreement when individuals fail to bring their concerns forward because of fear of being perceived as disagreeable, ignorant, incompetent, adversarial, risk averse, risk takers, worriers, or a whole range of other terms.

Probably the most stunning example of this occurred in a manufacturing company with which I am familiar. When the managers got together to discuss the process of implementing a new technology, the conversion date was quickly selected and a project schedule was developed for preparing to meet that deadline. Responsibilities were assigned to meet the agreed-on schedule. There was great enthusiasm for how well the process had worked, until major problems accompanied the transition.

Employees weren't adequately trained. The computer program that drove the new system was incompatible with programs being used in the rest of the operation, and the computer code that should have been rewritten wasn't. Links with other units using the old technology were lost. Suppliers hadn't been notified of projected down time, and distributors had not been informed of possible delays.

When the management group met to discuss what went wrong, almost every individual confessed to having had some concerns about the schedule in the planning meeting, but "since everybody else seemed to think it would work," reservations had not been voiced. They had manifested a modern-day "flight" trance by withholding their doubts.

Other times "flight" looks like avoidance. One group committed for several successive months to work on a particular project, but always managed to have an excuse for why it hadn't gotten to the project. When we finally discussed the topic, some deep differences emerged between members of the management team, and rather than have the courage to talk about those differences, they avoided the subject completely.

Still other times "flight" emerges as codependence. This may happen when a manager fails to address problems with employee performance. I've heard many excuses for this enabling behavior, and on the surface, they seem logical. They all spell fear (see box). In each case, the manager is enabling the poor behavior because he or she is afraid to address the problem. As we have already seen, perceived lack of time or resources is another common flight reaction.

Excuses That Mask Manager Codependence

"It's a bad time—we're really busy, and I haven't had time."

"It's a bad time—we're shorthanded, and I'm afraid she'll quit."

"I'm afraid others will be threatened and quit."

"I just hate to get on him—he's such a nice person."

"I hate to bring it up now—she's having a tough time at home."

I cannot overemphasize that these fight-or-flight responses are not happening on a cognitive level. They are occurring in autopilot or trance responses, which emerge from that part of our brain that can "hijack the thinking brain," as Goleman put it.

Our trances keep us from taking steps to change our behaviors and our way of relating to our fears, most often causing us to create self-fulfilling prophecies. When we aren't able to talk about our fears, we won't take the necessary action to prevent what we fear from occurring. When we don't take steps to do something differently, what we fear will come true. In *Leading from the Heart*, I said that I believe that, when we are afraid, the actions we take because of our fears actually create what it is that we most fear. I have seen it in my life. I have seen it in the lives of friends. I have seen it in organizations. If we cannot transcend the trance our fear creates, we will create what we fear.[8]

I worked in one organization in which there was a fairly common problem behavior that managers failed to address, "because we are so busy that we just don't have time." The problem behavior had become very common, and since people were not usually disciplined for doing it, employees had come to believe that it was OK. This meant that the incidence of occurrence increased dramatically.

We tracked how much of the manager's time was required if the procedure was performed properly. The answer was almost no time was required on an ongoing basis, but a little extra time and thoroughness were required in the training period. Then, we tracked how much of the manager's time was required if the process was done improperly. The answer this time, much to the managers' surprise, was three to four hours per occurrence! So, the second problem obviously was that the managers—those who thought they were too overworked to take time to address the problem—actually were spending many extra hours per week dealing with the fallout of the situation than would have been required to counsel the employees about performance problems in the first place.

Coupled with the increased incidence of the problem because employees had come to assume it wasn't a problem, managers were multiplying their workload many-fold. They actually reduced the amount of time they had, because they were afraid they lacked sufficient time to properly address the problem. In effect, much of their overwork was directly related to the inaction resulting from perceived lack of time. Their inaction was creating what they feared: more work. Their inaction became an action.

Still another thing they feared was that, if they started the employee counseling process and the employee's performance didn't improve, they might have to dismiss a person who otherwise was doing a good job in a time during which it had been difficult to hire qualified employees. Their failure to address the performance problems for fear of losing staff again created what they feared: this time, two exemplary employees left the company because they felt their good work wasn't appreciated since they were treated the same as people who didn't do their jobs properly.

So we come to another question: were lack of time and concern about turnover both disguises for deeper personal fears, maybe the fear of confrontation or the fear of having people not like us?

Ineffectiveness displayed by this group of managers really is quite common. That is why it is so important to organizational effectiveness, as well as personal well-being, to learn how to break these trances and bring our fears from the primitive part of our brains into our conscious and cognitive processes. It is critical for us to transform our relationship to fear by learning ways to bring fear into our consciousness, to accept it, to respect it, and to learn from it.

Why Choose Fear?

Why do people choose to be driven by fear when courage would be more appealing to most of us intellectually? Having spent several years in deep soul searching, personal growth and development, and other forms wrestling with my own fears so that I could live a fuller life, I will be the first to say that this work is not easy. As I do personal development work with clients, I repeatedly see their fears of looking at their fears. At the same time, I can see how their failure to do so is exacting a very high price from their organizations and their personal lives.

When we allow ourselves to function in fear-induced trances, we can sleepwalk through much of life's turmoil, having subconsciously convinced ourselves that life is easy, each question always has one right answer, and the "correct" course of action always is clear. We don't have to think about it. We need only shift to the appropriate trance and put ourselves on autopilot. Denial of fear is so comfortable—easy, natural, and believable to us when we're in it.

When we choose to acknowledge and accept fear, out of necessity, we must wake up. We must begin a conscious examination of each situation to determine which course supports our life purpose, our values, our intentions, and our growth. We must determine which actions will be in integrity with who we are on a soul level, not an ego one. The progression of the waking-up process usually includes an examination of who we are on a soul level, since that question is not likely to have surfaced when we were living in a trance state. As we are more aware, we may find ourselves increasingly compelled to examine. Often, this conscious realignment is agonizing. We may find ourselves locked deeply in a paradox that appears to grip us in a choice between different values we hold, that will require us to sustain the tension of not-knowing until we generate enough information about ourselves and the situation to take us beyond the either/or of the situation, which implies there is a right or wrong. When we have courage to examine the truth deeply, we almost always come to know there is no right or wrong and come to see truth in all possibilities.

Self-examination is not easy work. Having spent a number of years consciously doing it, I have almost come to believe that it actually gets harder. The deeper I go in my own work, the more ambiguous all of life seems. The black-and-white perspective of life has been replaced by an endless sea of differing shades of gray, and I am required to transcend habit countless times each day. The very moment I stop being conscious of my consciousness, it seems that without thinking I slip back into old fear-driven habits and trances.

Why on earth, then, would anyone consciously choose to live life being fully awake unless he or she is some sort of masochist? There are two answers: a personal one and an organizational one. The personal one is simple: we do it for our own growth. When we continue to go through life in a trance state, we stagnate. Life loses its color and excitement. We rob ourselves of the richness that life in its full complexity offers us. Our growth is integrally related to what I call "being awake" or off the autopilot-trance mode of living. Our development is the process of becoming more fully conscious, recognizing when we are in trances, and knowing how they limit us.

Our growth is rich with paradox. Courage is not needed when we aren't awake to more courageous options: we believe we have no choices. Occasionally, we may engage in an act of heroism that others will label *courageous*, but many such acts are automatic responses to a situation in which we didn't even consider not acting. Only when we begin to awaken to choice in our lives and our work does courage become an important quality to us.

We see a dramatic exemplification of the conscious courage as the hero faces torture and certain death at the end of the Academy Award-winning film *Braveheart*. William Wallace, a hero of the Scottish fight for independence, can save himself physically by simply pledging loyalty to the English king. Had he done so, he would have succumbed to a fear-induced trance concerned only with saving his neck. Instead, he acknowledges his fear and consciously chooses torture and death. To do otherwise, he says, would have robbed him of all that his life represented.

These kinds of decisions aren't choices we make on autopilot. They are choices of consciousness made in the conscious. They are choices to face our fear in favor of integrity with who we are on a soul level. They are the choices made by hundreds who acted to save Jews during Hitler's regime. They are the choices made by people like Stephen Biko to protest apartheid in South Africa. And, they are never made on autopilot.

The organizational reason for consciousness is compelling. In a time of rapid change, it is critical to be fully awake and in present time, attentive to what is happening now and open to a free flow of information that allows us to continuously reassess conditions and adjust consciously rather than reactively. When we are awake and in the present, we collectively discover possibilities that none of us could know in our fear-motivated isolation and compartmentalization—living and working based on what we have known in the past.

Fear, by nature, rarely exists in present time and space, and therefore it distracts us from being fully alert to conditions right now. Fear almost always is a function of a worldview that is reacting to events of the past or what we were taught was true in the past. A free flow of information is just as inhibited if we are afraid to share our perspectives or ideas because of possible or perceived retaliation as it is if we are afraid of hearing something that doesn't fit with our preferred view of the world. We *never* will function effectively or come anywhere near either our individual or collective potential as long as we are in denial of fear.

Transforming the Fear

- Futurists are predicting a new world in nearly every area of life. The pace of change is escalating and will become even more fluid, requiring us to adapt even more quickly to different roles in nearly every facet of our lives.
- The common threads in predictions for the future in every arena are wholeness, more openness and sharing, more mutual and self-acceptance, working together in flexible, fluid structures in continual cocreation.

- What is most telling of the prominence of fear in our work-places is that more truth is found in the unofficial meeting in the bathroom, the corridor, or the parking lot than where the decisions are being made.
- Our biggest organizational learning disability is our inability or unwillingness to recognize our fears and the destructive roles they lead us to play, both personally and organizationally.
- When we are afraid, we inevitably will work in a time dimension other than the present. The present is the only time dimension in which we can enact change or allow creativity to emerge.
- We experience fear when we feel powerless to change an outcome we believe will occur and by which we somehow feel threatened. Fears may be "obvious" and not so subtle or they may be deeper, subtle fears.
- Fear is the most primitive emotion. It is not logical, rational, thoughtful, or in any way intellectual. The thinking part of the brain developed much later. Our primitive fear mechanism produces automatic fight-or-flight trances that allow us to respond to threats *without thinking*.
- A new concept of security is evolving. We are moving from dependence on an organization to take care of us to one of interdependence, where we take care of ourselves *and* the organization and vice versa. We are evolving to be individual entrepreneurs, either within an organization or between organizations.
- Our worldview defines our limitations. When we are in one worldview, we will find another one threatening because it doesn't conform to our limitations. We always have to walk through fear to get to a new worldview.
- People choose fear because they are afraid to look at their fears. When we awaken from our trances, we must engage in a self-examination that requires conscious realignment with who we are on a soul level. This process is rich with paradox and confusion.

- We choose to go through the process personally because it enriches us and keeps us from stagnating. Organizationally, we choose to do it because the pace of change is so intense that it is critical for everyone to be fully awake, in the present, and able to respond consciously and creatively.

3

Emotional Competence

"We know the truth, not only by the reason,
but by the heart."

... BLAISE PASCAL

Despite all the hype in recent years about honoring diversity and learning from different perspectives, to admit that we fear a new situation or may need help is still tantamount to admitting incompetence. This avoidance isn't limited to organizations, although the impact is exponential in our work environment. As a culture, we are bereft of skills or courage to recognize, name, or process our emotions. We largely are a culture of emotional incompetents. And, sadly, that has been OK. We have sacrificed our emotional selves to the altar of science and intellect, and despite overwhelming evidence that our culture is sick, physically, mentally, emotionally, and spiritually as a result, our trances have kept us in a perverse acceptance of the situation.

Someone who has participated in 12-step programs recently said to me, "Denial is really comfortable when you're in it." Our denial of fear and the impact of compartmentalizing our lives by leaving our emotions at home has been so comfortable that we have preferred to become emotional zombies rather than learn to name, honor, and process our feelings, whether we think of them as good, bad, or indifferent. We are almost as inept at owning joy, delight, capability, satisfaction, and even love (except in the romantic sense) as we are fear, anger, sadness, resentment, or shame. How do you and coworkers respond to a colleague who is simply delighted and joyful about being at work? If the person is fairly new, we may dismiss the joy with, "You haven't worked here long enough," implying that eventually the attitude will be "fixed." If the person has been around for awhile, we may start asking what is going on in his or her private life, rather than to accept that someone might be feeling pure joy about work.

We have excused joy, denied fear, and largely ignored all of our emotions because we haven't the skills and understanding to competently accept and use them. While *The Joy of Work* may be another whole book, this one is about fear, because when we develop emotional competence in our relationship to fear, it has a transforming effect on our personal lives and our organizations. Fear is the most primitive emotion, and when we deny it, the resulting reactive trance sucks us into some of our most dysfunctional behaviors *without even knowing what is causing the behavior or even that it is happening.* Emotional competence enables us to begin to consciously use our emotions in all areas of our lives. To be able to live and work effectively, we must develop a level of competence that allows us to be whole and awake, experiencing what we are doing and feeling when we are doing and feeling it.

Stages of Competence

Emotional competence is a process, not an end point. As a process, we move through degrees of competence. We experience learning about ourselves and ourselves in relationship with others in several stages. First, we just begin to comprehend a concept. Later, we learn to apply that idea to a particular situation or set of conditions. Over time, we learn when the concept applies and to measure how well it is working. Eventually, we are able to apply the concept to different situations and maybe even teach the concept. Our ability to apply the concept in different situations is integrally intertwined with the ability to ask curious questions. These questions help us know how the new situation is like or different from those to which we have applied it in the past.

When I think about people who do a competent job at anything, the individuals who come to mind have a level of mastery that allows them to take a body of knowledge and generalize it to any situation. They don't depend on a set response (trance) to respond to a new situation. Instead, their level of capability allows them to "figure out what to do," even when they don't have the answer. In fact, developing competence at any endeavor seems to have as much to do with practice and knowing the right questions to ask as having the answer.

An individual may go to the doctor with a rash on her arm, for instance. The doctor could give her a salve to make the rash go away, but a competent doctor will ask her a number of questions that will provide insight into what is causing the rash. The result may be that the doctor suggests that the patient make a change in diet or laundry detergent or adjust the chemicals in her hot tub. A highly competent physician will ask about stressful work or family conditions or other situations that may generate a rash. That physician may end up giving the patient a salve, recommending a change in diet, *and* encouraging the patient to seek counseling to address the stressful situation. The highly competent physician knows the questions to ask to discover which, of a range of possibilities, applies to this case.

Now, let's take a look at how this competence building works for Karleen, a new manager of a particular manufacturing function. At first, Karleen just tries to learn the steps of the process and who does what. Over time, she begins to grasp what is entailed. Then, one day something isn't working right. In talking with people on the production team to learn more about the problem, Karleen discovers a different approach to completing the process. That stimulates both internal questioning and ques-

---

Stages of Competence

- Comprehend a concept.
- Apply the concept as presented to specific situations or conditions.
- Learn how to apply the concept to different situations.
- Ask questions and think about how to apply concept to unrelated situations.

---

tions to her coworkers about the underlying rules that allow both approaches to work. In the process of satisfying her curiosity, she discovers other approaches. Finally, at the weekly management meeting, as Karleen shares her discoveries, she and another manager discover applications for her discovery in his department. Her level of competence has evolved from just understanding what was going on, to analyzing and applying different approaches, to teaching, synthesizing, and generalizing what she had learned. Both her own questions and those of her fellow manager helped her grow in her learning (see box).

Developing Emotional Competence

When we look at emotional competence then, there also are degrees. Emotional incompetence is characterized by denial and avoidance of our own feelings and those of others. People exhibiting emotional incompetence are in a total trance state. On the rare occasions that an emotional reaction makes its way to the surface, these people make quick physical adaptations to camouflage that they actually may have feelings.

The first step in developing emotional competence is momentarily allowing an emotional reaction to surface and *recognizing it* before trying to suppress it. Even though the emotional reaction is recognized in this stage, it is treated as something shameful, something that needs to be changed or fixed. The reaction may be as simple as a crack in the voice or a spontaneous tear in the corner of the eye, or it may be an angry response that exceeds the severity of the occurrence that apparently stimulated it.

As their emotional competence evolves, people enter the stage in which they will likely continue to stifle the reaction but later bring it back to consciousness. They have come to accept their emotions as something from which to learn, and they spend some reflective time actually wondering about why they got so angry, why they found a lump in their throat when they were talking, or why their voice began to shake as they talked about what they wanted.

Why do we care about our emotional competence in an organizational setting? We cannot develop emotional competence in relating to others and their emotions until we have developed a comfortable level of self-acceptance about our own. If we judge our own reactions as inappropriate or shameful, those judgments inevitably will extend to others. We will miss a lot of important data if we stifle our own reactions or censor those of others. We will miss a lot of important data if we don't say what is important to be said because we allow our fear of what others will think to keep us from contributing fully. The company described earlier that ended up paying a million dollar ticket for a disastrous change in manufacturing technology because all of the managers were afraid to say what was on their minds knows the cost of emotional incompetence (see box on next page).

The next developmental stage is to feel what we feel when we feel it, accepting that whatever we are feeling is OK. We are nonjudgmental. There are no good feelings or bad feelings, right feelings or wrong feelings, just feelings. Only when we can be in touch with what we are feeling, when we are feeling it, can we begin to learn from it.

It is not uncommon in the fast-growth entrepreneurial companies that constitute most of my client groups to encounter a manager whose job has outgrown him or her. In fact, a major hurdle such companies must jump is the process of "profession-

Impact of Emotional Competence on Organization

Disown emotions; negative judgment about others showing emotions	→	No information; problems occur because data wasn't available
Acknowledge own emotions	→	No information; problems occur because data wasn't available
Explore own emotions	→	Information withheld; acknowledged only when problems occur
Learn from own emotions	→	Information withheld; acknowledged only when problems occur
Emotions explored together	→	Information begins to emerge
Consciously use emotions for learning	→	Information is sought; plan formulated to address fears; problems prevented before they occur

alizing" their management while continuing to find a useful place for those who built the company.

Those in positions that have outgrown them feel a great deal of fear, but it is virtually never addressed. Usually, they just let their stress level escalate out of control, while they try harder and harder to meet growing expectations, until a wake-up call of some kind occurs.

Others around them also have fears. Some wonder if they, too, are having difficulty keeping up with their expanding jobs but just don't know it. They fear they may be the object of bathroom and parking lot conferences. Owners appreciate the loyalty of those who helped build the company and are afraid they will seem ungrateful if they fire the employee. They also are afraid of the impact on the morale of others, who may wonder if they are next.

One manager whose job had outgrown her was under so much stress that you could almost see the chaos emanating from her office and her body. Alice wore a studied intensity that said strictly business, and she gave every sign of being quite professional. She always had the answer when someone asked her a question, but often the answers ended up being wrong. Errors were surfacing everywhere. As they did, Alice tried harder and harder to have a good explanation why something that looked like an error wasn't really. With time, even she could no longer deny that she simply couldn't handle the job.

That was about the time she and I started working together closely. Alice had been quite competent at the job she was hired to do. It just didn't exist anymore in the fast-growing company. She truly had the best interests of the company at heart. When I finally was able to get her to face her fears and share them with her management teammates, the magic of alchemy began. "I'm in over my head," she told them. "I'm afraid that I will make a mistake that will cost the company money. I'm afraid I will make a mistake that will get us in trouble with regulatory agencies. I'm afraid I will lose my job; I love working here, and I love all of you."

What followed was a combination of collective relief and compassion. The team no longer needed to walk on eggs, being careful not to say what everyone knew. They really could talk about the problems and put conscious analysis to solving them in a way that respected both Alice and their company values and set a precedent that eased concerns about their own positions.

First, the whole group supported Alice by acknowledging how difficult it had been for her to admit how overwhelmed she was. They demonstrated respect for her willingness to ask for help. Each offered to do whatever he or she could to assist Alice in learning to do her job differently, at the same time offering moral and emotional support whenever she needed it. That was really important, and it was something no one had been able to do until her fears were on the table.

Eventually, a group of managers sat with Alice and developed a plan for helping her learn aspects of her job that she didn't really understand. One manager had significant experience in Alice's area at another company and eagerly volunteered to take over some duties while she gained comfort with others. I, too, had worked in Alice's area for some years and had expertise that was important to the job that others in the company did not. I worked with her regularly as she learned that whole new area.

The last time I was at Alice's company, she was still learning, but everyone had confidence that she would make it. She looked years younger and much more relaxed. All the tension I used to feel when I walked into her office was gone. More important, now she was comfortable saying, "I don't know, but I will find out," or "I don't know how to do that, but if someone can get me started, I will be happy to do it."

Eventually, Alice may not make it. Many in her position do not. What sufficed for education and experience in a start-up that was hardly making a profit usually falls far short of what is needed to perform the same function in a $200 million company. But the emotional competence demonstrated by this whole team makes that always uncomfortable transition far more acceptable. Alice shared her feelings openly. The team accepted and respected them without judgment. Then all consciously could go about the cognitive task of solving the problem. None of these was happening before she shared her feelings. Far too often, this situation is dealt with as a bomb dropped on the manager at 5 o'clock Friday afternoon. No one feels good about it, and those left behind, wondering if they will be the next to go, certainly are less open to collaborative work relationships.

As our competence continues to develop, we are able to recognize an emotional reaction and stop in present time to explore it, having learned that the response most likely is not about what is occurring in current time and space. "Hmmm, that was a bit of a strong reaction, wasn't it? I wonder what that was about," we ask ourselves. We recognize that the response is not related to current events, and we help others who may have been angered or frightened by our response realize that what is going on most likely isn't about what is happening in the room at the moment.

Those who are most competent (and there are few of them) are comfortable experiencing and sharing both their own emotions and the emotions of others. They accept the other person's feelings, even if they may not agree with them. The emotionally competent don't try to "fix" the other person because they know emotions are normal and healthy. They don't give advice, although they may ask questions that help all concerned experience a deeper understanding of the other person's emotions. Like the person who is competent in other arenas, the most emotionally competent know that every situation is different. They respond appropriately to their own emotions and those of others, as they arise.

As we begin to develop emotional competence the most critical aspects are these:

- To be in the present time.
- To be mindful of what we are feeling as well as what we are thinking and to know the difference.
- To be mindful of reactions of others that may indicate their own emotional reactions.
- To accept and respect those emotions
- To recognize when we are going into an emotion-induced trance that was generated in another time and place, so that we can bring ourselves back into present time.
- To use our emotions to stimulate a reflective process of self-learning.

The emotionally competent are awake, aware, conscious, nonjudgmental, and courageous.

Our feelings provide important information that can help us be more healthy physically, mentally, intellectually, and spiritually. Unfortunately, most of us are so uncomfortable with both our own feelings and those of others that we have a deep and unhealthy fear of that most essential part of ourselves. Even though the most critical aspects of emotional competence are to be in present time and mindful and accepting of our emotions, it is easy to slip back into a habit-induced trance. We cannot perform the mental and physical functions we are at work to do if we aren't "here." Until we snap ourselves out of the trance, we cannot be fully conscious and attentive to the work at hand.

(Probably the easiest way to pull oneself out of a trance is to take two or three deep, diaphragmatic breaths. As simple as it is, the quick and simple deep-breathing exercise almost always pulls us out of our trance and into present time.)

As our emotional competence develops further, we are grateful for whatever the feeling is and learn to use it as a source of introspection, reflection, and learning about ourselves. Personally, as I have learned to accept and appreciate feelings that I didn't like in myself, I have experienced my most profound revelations and sources of growth. At the same time, it took incredible courage to accept, appreciate, and meditationally explore feelings about which I felt shame, embarrassment, and even a lack of integrity. This deep soul searching hasn't been popular in our quick-fix culture. More often than not, we just pop a pill and make the pain go away. When we avoid the reflection, contemplation, meditation, or whatever word you prefer to mean deep and meaningful soul searching, we miss the gifts of learning and stifle our capacity to feel all of our emotions.

Components of Emotional Competence

The first component of emotional competence is to be present. This means that we are awake, fully aware of what we are doing, thinking, and *feeling* when we are actually doing, thinking, and feeling it. We come to recognize our fear reactions and our trances. We become conscious of the need to take a few deep breaths to bring ourselves into present time. We are willing to admit that we are uncomfortable about something being said.

Stages of Emotional Competence

- Ignore emotions. Suppress them when they erupt. Ignore any emotional reactions of others; change the subject if necessary.

- Allow the emotional reaction to surface and recognize it before trying to suppress it. Ignore any emotional reactions of others; change the subject if necessary.

- Allow the emotional reaction to surface, recognize it before trying to suppress it, then come back to it later and reflect on what was being felt at the time. Still don't acknowledge emotional reactions in others, but wonder about what the person was feeling.

- Allow the emotional reaction; feel what you feel when you feel it. Allow others to experience their emotions as they feel them.

- Be willing to use your own emotions to learn about yourself, either on your own or confidentially.

- Be willing to talk about your own emotional reaction when it happens more openly; be willing to open the door for others to talk about their emotional reactions *if they choose to do so.*

- Be willing and committed to practicing emotional competence, knowing that it takes time to grow into.

A management team I worked with did a process to identify the signs of each other's trance states. The executive director was surprised to learn that one of his trance reactions inhibited team input. Although this man really wanted their input, whenever he became uncomfortable about something that was being said, he would reach down and pull up his socks. Everyone on the team identified that this action meant "change the course of your remarks" (their own trance responses) because the boss didn't like them. Everyone knew this except the person doing it! Before people were even able to finish their comments, they knew he had gone into his disapproval trance.

Acceptance of the emotions of others without judgment is the second component of emotional competence. This means self-acceptance as well as the acceptance of what others are feeling. Acceptance doesn't imply agreement, it simply means understanding what the other person is feeling without judging that it is right or wrong or silly. We also understand what we are feeling in relationship to the other's feelings. When we honor our feelings and the feelings of others, we do not try to convince others that what they are feeling is wrong. Nor do we try to fix them by getting them to look at the situation a different way. It simply means that we accept what the person is experiencing right now. That is where we really can work together rather than from some fictional predisposition that we are all OK.

In dynamic organizations, a high level of involvement by everyone is critical, and the owners of the company usually understand that. However, I regularly encounter significant self-censoring by employees, who are afraid they will get fired if they say what they know. Because I know the owners want involvement, I could say that the employee's reactions are silly; the owners want to hear what they have to say.

That is not an emotionally competent approach. The person is frightened. If I say the fears are silly, that will only make the person afraid to talk with me. When I accept that someone is afraid to speak up, then we can engage in a dialogue that helps both of us better understand the fear and move beyond it. Too often we try to sell our ideas without first understanding the emotional roots to resistance. Acceptance of one another's feelings almost always opens wider the door to each other's ideas.

The third component of emotional competence is to be open to talking about and coming to understand (processing) our own emotional reactions and those of others. A respectful and open inquiry that values the emotional reaction as a source of important information to each of us will be of benefit, both personally and to our collective organizational endeavor.

When I worked with one small company, it was the third or fourth attempt in as many years to move the firm into a team

---

Components of Emotional Competence

- *Be in the present:* fully awake, fully aware of what we are doing, thinking, and feeling when actually doing, thinking, and feeling it.

- *Accept the emotions of yourself and others without judgment:* honoring the feeling without agreement or trying to "fix" the other person.

- *Be open to processing emotions:* process both your own emotions and those of others, respectfully and openly; respect information so obtained and use it to improve decisions.

- *Be willing and committed:* use your own emotions and those of others as a source of self-learning, using a reflective or contemplative process.

- *Practice:* emotional competence is not an end point; it is a learning process that goes on forever.

---

operation, so there was great cynicism about the chances of the success of this project. I had to begin with just such an inquiry into people's emotions about the project. I met with the owners and top managers and discussed what they were afraid of this time and what they had been afraid of in the past that kept the earlier attempts from being successful. People were afraid to stick their necks out this time because, in the past, even though the owners said they envisioned involvement, the moment things didn't go as they wanted, they would take back control. Worse yet, sometimes people had been fired. That told me that it was essential for me to work with the owners on how to interact when they became frightened. It also told me that it was essential for them not to give even an illusion of wresting back control, which would have been taken as a clear invitation to the employees for a "been there and done that and don't care to go there again" reaction. And rightly so. This was critical information to the success of the project.

In the end, the project was successful. In fact, it was so successful that the owners bought two other companies to run because the team was doing such a good job of running things that, as one owner told me, "There wasn't anything for me to do any more."

The fourth component of emotional competence is the willingness and commitment to use both our own emotional reactions and those of others as a source of self-learning. We accomplish this through a reflective, contemplative, or meditational process. We then must use the learning that comes from such soul-searching to bring a deeper level of awareness to future interactions. The introspective process also invites grappling with the more existential questions of life and how they relate to our everyday work. The product of such reflective exercises is to shed light on a spectrum of components that drive our decisions but are rarely mentioned.

For instance, an angry outburst or an impassioned speech with a cracking voice may become the source of both individual and collective soul-searching that reveals a connection with an earlier initiative during which an individual was forced to take actions that violated his or her personal values. This is important information from which those participating in the process can find gold. They may discover that they need to be more conscious about designing programs within the company's stated values, as well as becoming more aware of the need to ask people if they are comfortable with what they have been asked to do. This is critical information for a company to have if its new undertakings are going to be ones employees can really get behind.

One company even took the existential questions to an organizational level. When one executive said he was afraid that their company would not stay in business if they worked within their current corporate values, another stimulated a vigorous dialogue by responding, "If we can't operate within our values, do we deserve to stay in business?" Until we face our fear and talk about questions of deeper meaning, our organizational values will be words on a plaque in the lobby. Raising these questions and the implications of the dialogue that ensues will begin bringing those values to life.

When an individual has the courage to speak up, to invite reflection about organizational values, a parallel personal introspective process may generate further questions. What are my values? What causes me to violate my values? What can I do to help myself and others be conscious about working the way the company's values say we will work and bring values into the decision-making arena more? Is this a company in which I should be working?

Both personally and collectively, the deep questions that emotional competence invites are ones that bring life and meaning to us individually and to the vision and values process we have been going through for the last 20 years in many businesses.

The final component of emotional competence is practice. Emotional competence is not an end point—it is a process that goes on forever. We get better only by practicing it. The first time a person has the courage to say what he or she is feeling may be incredibly uncomfortable, both for that person and those who are listening. The pregnant silence that follows may be painful. There may be those who don't even want to acknowledge the remark and choose to distract the group by moving ahead with what is on the agenda. Over time, though, when a group has the courage to stay with the discomfort, to use the pregnant silence to explore what each of them is feeling, and then to honestly and openly accept the other's feelings, the quality of meetings and the quality of the workplace will be transformed.

The Difference Between Thinking and Feeling

Implicit in knowing what we are feeling is understanding the distinction between feelings and thoughts. When people say, "I feel *that* . . . ," more often than not what follows is a thought. "I feel *that* I would like for you to take on more responsibility for getting the work done" isn't a feeling at all. It is a thought about what I would like to see happen, and it is probably important information

Feelings

Admiration	Fulfillment	Openness
Adventurousness	Gladness	Pain
Anger	Gratitude	Peace
Capability	Grief	Rage
Compassion	Happiness	Resentment
Confusion	Hatred	Respect
Courage	Hope	Revenge
Creativity	Humiliation	Sadness
Depression	Hurt	Satisfaction
Devastation	Inspiration	Shame
Disappointment	Irritation	Sympathy
Embarrassment	Jealousy	Terror
Empathy	Joy	Trust
Enthusiasm	Loneliness	Vulnerability
Fear	Loss	Willingness
Frustration	Love	

to be communicated. However, the feeling would be more appropriately communicated as, "I am *angry* because it seems like I do far more than my share of the work around here." Or, the feeling may be one of being frustrated, irritated, disappointed, hurt, or afraid (see box).

Similarly, many people confuse judgment for feeling. For example, someone may say, "I feel good that we are talking about this." *Good* is a qualitative, judgment word, not a feeling word. What the individual may be trying to communicate may be, "I *think* it is *good* that we are talking about this, and I *feel happy* about that." Or, the person may think it is good to be talking, but *feel* uncomfortable, uneasy, relieved, or delighted about doing so. We cannot really be aware of what we are feeling until we distinguish our thoughts and judgments from our feelings. We cannot competently transform fear or any other emotion that throws us into a trance-induced reactive state until we distinguish it from the products of our intellect. Fear is a feeling, and until we can feel it—not think about it—we can't begin to develop competence in processing it. Instead, we will be sucked into an intellectual trance that will do one of two things. It will give us the illusion that our fears have been "addressed" or we will focus on the not-so-subtle fears rather than deeper and more meaningful fears that will stop our work processes.

Awaking from Our Trances

We are largely a culture that is sleepwalking through life and work. The reason we want emotional competence is to help us wake up and learn to work together consciously. Living in a fear-induced trance is relatively easy—until we get a wake-up call. Organizationally, that may come when a competitor begins taking major market share, taxpayers fail to pass a "routine" funding measure, or a consultant's analysis reports significant organizational dysfunction. Personally, it occurs with a "surprise" divorce, a premature heart attack, or the death of a colleague or close contemporary.

A lifetime of trance-induced denial has left most of us emotionally incompetent, and we respond to a wake-up call as quickly as possible, modifying one of our working trances just enough to get us out of the pain of the moment. Then we revert quickly to autopilot. We have become the "Prozac society" that just wants the pain to go away so we won't have to either feel our emotions or experience the growth that integrally relates to the wake-up experience. Our failure to address our emotional pain and grow with it can make us physically sick as well. Finally, some of the medical community is beginning to see the important role of the physician in encouraging people to do their spiritual and emotional healing work, in conjunction with undergoing the prescribed medical treatment of physical symptoms.[1]

The Stress Reduction and Relaxation Program at the University of Massachusetts Medical Center has been hugely successful for many years in assisting doctors as they work with their patients on an integrative level rather than simply a physical one. Doctors send patients suffering from a range of illnesses, including headaches, high blood pressure, back pain, heart disease, cancer, and AIDS, to learn meditation and other techniques that help them live mindfully in the present. The impressive statistics that the program has amassed over the years would lead one to believe this work might actually be a wonder drug.[2]

When consciously assessing all data, including emotional information, an organization might spend days or weeks of soul searching before responding. The individual might spend months consciously grieving a personal loss, a practice that is nearly intolerable to those around us in this culture. The inner work required to develop emotional maturity and competence is reflective and meditative, causing us to contemplate the existential questions of life. None of this easily fits into our "make the pain go away *now*" culture.

When we suppress our pain, grief, loss, sadness, fear, anger, or any other "negative" emotions, we simultaneously contain our positive ones. Our incompetence in dealing with the downside of our emotional life robs us of the upside. We lose the peace, joy, love, and passion for life, along with our creativity, satisfaction, and capability. Our fear-driven trances take us closer and closer to stagnation: unable to experience either pain or enjoyment. Just perpetual numbness. As we disconnect the emotional part of ourselves, we stop growing and gradually draw more and more within ourselves. We lose the spontaneity, flexibility, creativity, and passion for responding to new challenges. Our options become more and more limited. Over time we appear, both to ourselves and to others, to be spiritually dead. Furthermore, we've become so comfortable with this kind of existence that we don't want to be awakened from our trances.

The Great Divide

To become emotionally competent, we must first acknowledge and name our emotions. Our emotions are tools. When we deny or ignore them, we steal from ourselves a powerful tool for learning and growth. Denying and ignoring emotions will not make them go away—it simply establishes a conflictual relationship within ourselves. We are fighting our emotions. They are seeking to get our attention to communicate something, and we are fighting them in what becomes an increasingly futile attempt to make them go away. They will not go away. They may choose a different manifestation—irritability, a short temper, a headache, stomach problems, or a heart attack—but they won't go away. As we expend more and more energy fighting ourselves, we become exhausted, depressed, and eventually physically sick.

When we deny our emotions, we create schisms in our lives. We compartmentalize and divorce a part of ourselves. The division sucks energy from us wherever we are divided. Surrendering the fight opens us to incredible potential as we begin regaining our own personal power from within ourselves. The simple act of being in the present moment, knowing what we are feeling and saying instantly begins the process of making us whole again. We cannot begin to heal or integrate what we don't know exists.

Two different situations come to mind that demonstrate how being able to accept emotion, appreciate it, and use it for personal introspection can allow us to grow, heal, and be both more effective and more fulfilled.

Not long ago, I found myself having sexual feelings about a man with whom I had a professional relationship, and it felt most inappropriate to me both because it violated my professional ethics and because he was in a committed relationship. I resisted my feelings for a long time. Finally, though, I surrendered. What I felt was what I felt. When I accepted what I was feeling *without judgment*, I could begin to understand and heal the part of me that spawned the feeling.

I spent several hours reflecting deeply about what in this man was so appealing to me. Much to my surprise, I didn't discover a steamy tryst, but instead realized that the joyful, light, and fun-loving nature of this man reminded me of my lost childhood. When I was able to accept what I first felt was a sordid side of myself and use it as a source of personal introspection, I rediscovered what had been a continuing theme in my life: I discovered that I needed to learn to play. *More important* to me, I was able to make this discovery in a way that respected my own integrity and my colleague's relationship commitment. I wonder how many sexual harassment situations could be avoided if the perpetrators would choose to use their feelings to instigate an inner self-discovery process. Instead of being compelled to act on their feelings physically or verbally, by choosing such a process, what might they learn needed to be healed within themselves?

The second situation involved a particularly competent corporate officer. When I began coaching her, she complained of extreme frustration: she was unable to focus on important projects because the day-to-day activities already consumed more time than a normal work week. She was simply not willing to sacrifice any more of her personal and family time to take on projects that even she admitted were crucial.

After we worked together a while, she was able to finally admit that she was afraid she wouldn't be able to do the crucial projects if she got to them. She then was able to admit that most of the activities that consumed her time could be delegated to other individuals, but her trance-induced protective strategy had used them as an excuse to keep her from taking on projects she found threatening. Coming to this consciousness allowed her both to begin off-loading many activities and determining what additional background and research she needed to prepare her for more critical work.

Whatever our emotions are trying to tell us, they carry a message about how we can generate more internal power and energy by becoming more whole. When we have fear and avoid it by denial, we divide ourselves, we are less whole. When we have fear, but we acknowledge it and learn what we must do to move toward it and grow from it, we come together and are more whole.

When we are emotionally scattered and fragmented, both personally and collectively, we cannot do our best work. Emotions give us important data—data that should be mined for the gold, not ignored. When we ignore major pieces of data that our emotions provide, we are not making our best decisions. When we stifle our creativity as a function of stifling our emotions, we limit our personal and organizational possibilities and potential.

One young manager I know recently shared with me his frustration at having to screen out every bit of data that wasn't tangible. "I feel extremely limited in my decision making by having to stick to what I can tangibly see and measure. I have to leave out a lot of important intangible information, but I don't know how my boss would react to me bringing in that information which I have and want to consider."

When we purge our organizations of emotional data, we rob them. We rob them of decisions made with all the pertinent data. We rob them of creativity. As we put the lid on all emotions, we rob them of energy and enthusiasm. Furthermore, in addition to robbing our organizations of effectiveness, the compartmentalization and inner schisms we are experiencing, coupled with the physical illnesses to which they make us vulnerable, are costing us billions of dollars in health-care costs as we invite ourselves to be sicker and sicker. Our organizational response has been cost-containment programs and cost sharing when it should have been organizational healing.

The choice to heal ourselves and our organizations begins with a choice to change our relationships to our emotions, especially fear. Because fear is a core emotion that underlies our other "negative" emotions (anger, frustration, humiliation, shame, guilt, jealousy, hurt), we heal the schism in ourselves, and between ourselves and our work, when we respectfully accept our fear.

Transforming the Fear

- The denial of fear and the compartmentalization of our emotions from the rest of our lives has left us emotional zombies, sleepwalking through life. Our incompetence in dealing with the "downside" emotions has robbed us of the "upside."
- Emotional competence is a process, not an end point.
- The most critical aspects of emotional competence are

    To be in the present time.

    To be mindful of what we are feeling as well as what we are thinking and to know the difference.

    To be mindful of reactions of others that may indicate their emotional reactions.

    To accept and respect those emotions.

    To recognize when we are going into an emotion-induced trance that was generated at another time and place, so that we can bring ourselves back into present time.

    To use our emotions to stimulate a reflective process of self-learning.

- The deep questions that emotional competence invites are ones that bring life and meaning to us individually and to our organizational vision and values.
- Our emotions are tools. When we deny or ignore them, we steal a powerful tool for learning and growth from ourselves. Denying and ignoring our emotions will not make them go away—they simply establish a conflictual relationship with ourselves, sucking energy from us wherever we are divided.

4

Resisting Emotional Competence

"You gain strength, courage, and confidence by every experience in which you really stop to look fear in the face. You are able to say to yourself, 'I lived through this horror. I can take the next thing that comes along.' You must do the thing you think you cannot do."

ELEANOR ROOSEVELT, "This 'n That"[1]

Despite the positive effects of being awake to our emotions, most of our culture consciously chooses to live life not being fully awake. Why? Why would we want to live in a trance rather than be fully awake in our lives?

The most obvious answer is that most of those who choose to live life in a trance are not doing so consciously. Because most of our existence (and it is an existence, not a life) has been in a trance, we are not aware that there are other possibilities. It has been said that a fish doesn't know it is in water until it isn't, because that is the only thing it knows. It cannot know water until it knows other possibilities exist, such as living in air. Those who have never experienced being awake in life don't know that any other option exists. Only when we begin to be awake for even short periods of time do we begin to understand that one could actually begin to live that way, maybe even most of the time.

Even though many would choose to be awake, some people have chosen to sleep through life. They have emerged into a wakeful, conscious life, and they have chosen to go back to a trance state. Why would someone do that?

Being awake is hard work. It is not a quick fix; the more we learn, the more we know there is to learn. As we begin listening to our emotions and learning things about ourselves and our feelings, we may not like what we see or hear about us when we are awake. In a culture of pain avoidance and quick fixes, all of these may be reasons why we wouldn't want to choose to live our lives being fully awake.

These are the more obvious reasons why people wouldn't want to be awakened from their trances. Deeper reasons hold us locked in the death grip of fear. As long as we sleepwalk our way through our lives, we aren't responsible. When we regain our inner power, more accountability and less blaming is required from us, and we stop being victims. When we are awake and committed to living our lives instead of being driven through life by fear, we know that the power of our intentions to face our fears will allow us to move through that very same fear, transforming it into a learning device instead of being its slave. Yet, at the very same time, we must surrender to the emptiness of not knowing *how* the learning will manifest.

Physician and motivational speaker Elliott Dacher encourages physicians to become more actively involved in encouraging and supporting their patients' spiritual development as a critical part of the healing process. He has said, "Powerlessness has street value."[2] He is absolutely right. That's what the old saying "Misery loves company" is all about. Nothing bonds people more quickly than shared wounds.

In fact, theologian Caroline Myss, who teaches about the emotional and spiritual causes of physical illness, believes that one of the main reasons people won't heal is because victims know that, when they stop being victims, their bond to other victims (many of whom are close friends and family) will break. On some level, they actually choose to be physically ill rather than give up their powerlessness and the network of commiserating victims that goes with it.[3]

One way to understand what Myss is saying is through the use of archetypes. Archetypes are metaphorical roles common to the human experience and through which each of us must move in order to grow. They often are based on a myth, fairy tale, or occasionally real-life occurrences. The Magician and the Orphan that we visited earlier are archetypes. The word *orphan* brings with it a certain set of understandings. This is how archetypes help us. They give us a universal understanding of what is going on beyond the literal events of current time and place.

Throughout our lives, we live through many such timeless sequences. At work, speaking up for troubled coworkers may equate to the archetypical myth of slaying the dragon. We learn more about developing courage to be the workplace "hero" as we learn what the dragon slayer did. Stories often help us learn about the circumstances of our own lives by presenting archetypes from which we can learn.

Myss believes that the story of Christ's crucifixion is an archetype that we must all live. It represents betrayal, the consequent suffering, and finally the granting of forgiveness that each of us must learn to get on with our lives and evolve spiritually. Myss says that most of us get stuck in the suffering stage. We aren't able to move on because forgiveness would require us to leave the past behind, and most of us gain too much value from our victimhood to be willing to let go of it.[4] Our victimhood locks us into fear, as we come to believe we are powerless to change an outcome and are threatened by the inevitable.

Emotional competence requires us to bring whatever emotion we are experiencing to our consciousness, learn from it, and learn to move beyond it. When the emotion is fear, that frequently requires us to psychically go back to the pain that caused us to develop the fear trance in the first place. We learn what from that situation applies to current time. When we receive the gift of learning the experience held and grant forgiveness where necessary, we finally can move beyond the fear. Emotional competence gives back our power in our relationship with fear.

Jon Kabat-Zinn, director of the Stress Reduction Clinic at the University of Massachusetts Medical Center, has helped thousands of people transform their relationship to pain, stress, and fear, using a set of practices that develop mindfulness. He explains how mindfulness can help us to change our relationship with fear: "When you move in close to your fears and observe them as they surface in the form of thoughts, feelings, and bodily sensations, you will be in a much better position to recognize them for what they are and know how to respond to them appropriately. Then you will be less prone to become overwhelmed or swept away by them or to have to compensate in self-destructive or self-inhibiting ways"[5]

Shifting to Inner Motivation

Emotional competence requires us to give up being the victim of fear. When we do that, we must stop being motivated by people, actions, and beliefs outside of us. We must look inside and see what our Higher Self really feels, thinks, and believes, not what our parents, spouse, friends, or boss tell us. When we turn to our Higher Self, what we learn may require us to believe, think, and act differently than many around us. Going inside invites us to assess our values and determine our life's purpose, then to use those inner guidance systems to make decisions. This requires courage.

When we awaken from our trances and begin living from Higher Being, we may discover that our slumbering souls have plans for our lives that are different from the ones we had. Our soul may remember that it came into this life with a specific humanitarian purpose, which has nothing to do with the executive suite with a view, the 4,000-square-foot house, the Mercedes or

BMW in its garage, or sending the children to the most expensive universities. When we wake up, we may discover that our soul has much simpler material requirements because life's rewards are now experienced in achieving our higher purpose and developing higher levels of consciousness.

As long as we are asleep, we can pretend that all there is to life is the position, the house, the car, status universities, and having fun. When we are awake, we realize that to heal our lives we are compelled to live the life that is ours to live, not the life that society, our parents, neighbors, spouse, business partners, or the folks at the country club believe we *should* lead. Emotional competence means that we look at it all and struggle with it. We sustain the emptiness and the fear that often comes with the spiritual wrestling match until we reach a level of clarity from our soul about what right action to take.

When we are awake, we come to know that we have an internal guidance system that was provided to counsel us in our decisions and direction in life. Fear is an integral part of that system. Letting go of who we have believed we were to make room for who we really are is one of the hardest things that we must do in life, and to be whole, we must do it. This requires emotional competence. It requires us to know what we feel and to be OK feeling that—good, bad, ugly, or indifferent. And it requires that we not let our fears stop the process until it is complete.

Upsetting the Existing Systems

Over the last five years, I've personally peeled away layer after layer of who I believed I was. Each time an almost crazy-making push-pull wrestled within me. I found it impossible to say "no" to what I now knew the purpose of my life was. At the same time, I faced deeper fear about what it would mean for my life—the consequences I would face—as I consciously chose to act out of my own integrity and not the *shoulds* of the world. As I write this, I continue to wrestle with one more layer of belief systems that drives another set of habits about who I believed I was.

Every time I come to this point, I know that some people who have been dear to me will not be comfortable with the real me. They have grown to like the person I was when I was asleep in the part of my life that interacted with them. Each time, some activities my sleeping self enjoyed will not be compatible with who I really am.

Without knowing that I was grappling with the same issue, in the last month, at least 10 people have confessed to me that they were feeling the need to let go of the person they thought they had been. Each has a story about how that will affect his or her relationships, families, work, or income. Yet each has expressed the same feeling that I have experienced; once I am awake in life, I cannot fail to do what is mine to do! If I and they had not developed the courage and emotional competence to stay with the process, even when it has been extremely painful, we would have stopped growing and gone back to sleep.

Challenging the Dominant Culture

When I was sleepwalking through life, I didn't struggle with these things. I just did what the culture told me I *should* do, literally, *without thinking about it.* Oh, I did overanalyze decisions. *Should* I stay with my current company with more money and career advancement opportunities? Or *should* I take a job that would allow me more time with my family? But, when I was asleep, it never crossed my mind to ask, "Why am I here on this Earth? What is my purpose? What work must I do that will change the course of humankind?" My life trance was designed to keep me from facing the fear of the consequence of the answers I might get, so my programming with these existential questions was locked away from me.

Unless we have surrounded ourselves with people who are awake, which isn't something most sleepwalkers do, the reaction of our friends, families, and coworkers as we begin to ask questions for which their trances have no frames of reference may range from discomfort to wrath. As long as we are all asleep, we can relate to each other, trance to trance; but when even one person wakes up, it is likely to begin making others aware that something may not be quite right in their own lives. Sleepwalkers usually don't want to look at themselves, so their protective trance tells them to take control, react angrily, attempt to convince the waking person that something is terribly wrong with *them*. As long as the sleepwalkers' trance keeps them in the illusion that the problem is somewhere other than inside them, they don't have to start the soul searching that will awaken them from their trance.

A close friend of mine spent several days with her sister during a period in which it appeared that her sister's husband would die from advanced-stage alcoholism. At the end of a two-week hospital stay, the man had "dried out," and finally he had come to the realization that he must give up drinking. As a consequence of good personal therapy and a 12-step program, in the weeks that followed, he started to be healthy. Then, she reported what happened in the rest of the immediate family. As he began to be healthy, the dependent-codependent system that the family had sustained for many years began to break down. His health required each of the other family members to become more healthy, and they didn't like that. They would have to do their own inner work. So, the family members began to sabotage his sobriety! It appears that they would rather have him dead than healthy, if his health required them to awaken from their trances and look at themselves.

Similarly, when I began making decisions based on what I knew was healthy for me, I was shocked to discover that my friends didn't share my happiness in discovering new-found direction and peace. Not only didn't they share it, my very best friend was downright angry. She wrote me a vicious letter telling me how selfish I was because I wasn't going to live my life the way she thought I should.

When that didn't dissuade me, she sent her husband (who also was a good friend) to "talk some sense" into me. He said he thought I'd been enraptured, implied that was bad, and thought I needed to come back to my senses. What *enraptured* really means is to be overtaken by a lofty emotion, such as ecstasy. Being awake did feel pretty lofty compared to how I'd lived most of my life, and to say I was ecstatic about it is probably not too strong. Where we disagreed was that I thought that it was good that I was awake and making decisions that were healthy for me instead of doing what everyone else thought I should do. Not unlike the situation with the alcoholic and his family, some of my friends would have preferred that I sleepwalk through life, rather than wake up and begin making decisions that nudged them in their trance worlds.

Denial often is part of the early stages of any growth process. For those who are still sleeping through life, a wake-up call may feel like a bucket of cold water in the face in the middle of the night. They just want to go back to sleep and pretend it didn't happen, but they're awake now—and the pillow is still wet. Even if they do go back to sleep, the next morning the pillow still will be wet, to remind them things are not the way they have believed they were. Because emotional competence is about accepting both the feelings we have and those of others, it is important to remember that it also means accepting their denial. It doesn't mean that *we* have to go back to sleep.

I love these people, and I understand that their reactions were their way of showing love to me while running from the fear of their own self-examination. I didn't try to get them to wake up, and I didn't get discouraged—let my courage to live my life be sucked from me. I listened to my internal guidance system rather than the externally motivated cultural one.

My work repeatedly has brought me face to face with people who have begun to wake up enough to know they need to do something differently in their lives, but they are afraid to challenge the cultural norms. So, they continue to experience various kinds of distress, ranging from addictions to health problem to lethargy, rather than follow their internal guidance system. Their internal anguish not only caused them internal problems but, in most cases, had an impact on their families and their coworkers, which they had preferred to ignore.

As I reflect on it, I realize that a major component of my consulting practice has been that of encourager, the one who helps others to find the courage to listen to their own internal spiritual guidance in the face of an externally motivated world. I have helped them name their fears and move toward them. I have helped them recognize when they are in a trance and make denial at least uncomfortable, if not impossible.

Sometimes, that involved leaving a job, an especially challenging move since I usually am working with the company owners. Occasionally, it involved helping people have the courage to take a lateral move or even a demotion because they didn't like a particular job they had been doing. Other times, I have helped managers discover the courage to lead the people who report to them in a less directive way. When they began waking up, they knew that the way they had been working simply was out of touch with what they had come to know was right on a deeper inner level. Still other times, I have helped managers, like Alice, admit that they were in over their heads and helped them find the courage to ask for help.

Unless someone has had a serious wake-up call, like a sobering illness, an unexpected divorce, or death of a close contemporary, coming to consciousness always is difficult and almost always takes a period of internal healing during which the individual comes to trust his or her inner guidance deeply. Sometimes, as much as two years pass before an individual who admitted that a change must occur was willing to take on the fear of telling a business partner or spouse.

The Power of Saying the Words

It is a most mysterious process to me how individuals can struggle about what to do for months and even years, but the moment they find the courage to stand up before even one or two other people and face the fear of speaking for their Selves, that wise inner part of each of us, everything changes. They no longer struggle with *whether* to do what they know is right. The question then shifts to *how* to do what they know is right.

This is the power of emotional competence. It is the power of moving toward our fear, and I find that, until we say the words to others, the fear is not real to us. Only by saying the words about what our deep fears are do we regain the power to transform our relationship to them from denial to inner power.

Doing it the first time is the hardest. After a lot of practice, people actually can come to recognize their own fear trances fairly quickly, wake up from them, and say, "What is it that I am afraid of? What does that fear have to teach me so that I can move toward it?" Each time that we move toward our fear, we gain the inner peace and courage that allows us to do it more easily the next time.

On New Year's Eve 1992, I pledged to myself that I no longer was going to let fear be in the driver's seat in my life. I made this quiet pledge to myself, and unlike many New Year's resolutions, I knew that keeping this pledge was essential to the life of my soul. As I moved through the first few months, I found myself looking at personal issues from childhood that I had put away for most of my life because I was afraid of looking at them. Then, I found myself turning away work that I felt lacked integrity with my soul, even though I was afraid I wouldn't be able to earn a living. I even faced the fear of taking time off from my consulting work to write my first book, even when I was afraid I wouldn't be able to write a book.

What I discovered, when I began to notice, was how often I reacted to situations from trances born of some unspoken fear. Opportunities about which I one time might have said, "That doesn't interest me," or "I don't like to do those kind of things," I now came to recognize represented fear of trying something new or possibly discovering I might like something about which I had once had negative judgment. I even realized how often I'd censored activities, in the name of just exercising good judgment, because they weren't safe; yet, actually, they were being done regularly by many people, so they couldn't be *that* unsafe. It didn't seem to matter in what area of my life I recognized that fear was stopping me from living fully, when I moved toward the fear, I gained a self-confidence and energy that propelled me forward in the rest of my life.

A Rock Ledge and a Waterfall Transformed My Relationship to Fear

I began to take on physical challenges as well. I had spent much of my 40-plus years being a physical "fraidy cat" who simply didn't try things if they were physically challenging, and I distinctly disliked any kind of "creepy-crawly thing." I remember my husband watching me join a group of mostly adolescent boys as I pulled myself up a 15-foot rock ledge by a rope and slid down a waterfall into a pool of salamanders. "I can't believe you did that," he said, adding, "I'm really proud of you." With tears of joy in my eyes, my response was, "I can't believe I did it either. I wouldn't do it again for anything, and I am *really* glad I did it."

I cannot begin to explain to anyone who has not done it, how empowering an experience like that can be. Like Eleanor Roosevelt's quote at the beginning of this chapter, when I'd lived through "that horror," I could "take the next thing that comes along." Since then, I have faced many challenges, and I have done many mental flashbacks to what it was like to be hanging by a rope over that pool, ready to shoot down the waterfall, and I have known that if I could do that, I could do anything. It seemed to signal a change in my life.

Later in that year, I returned from a national meeting, knowing that my work was much bigger than the small geographic and profile parameters I had put around it in the past. So, I faced my fear about what that would mean to my relationship with my husband. As I found the courage to talk about it with him, I knew I had crossed a bridge in acknowledging and accepting my own life's purpose, as well as the fears associated with what pursuing it might mean. Having faced the fear of talking about what I wanted, we were able to talk about what we would do to maintain the relationship in the face of expected changes. I could now move forward with the support and encouragement of my partner instead of being held back out of fear that he would be upset. Having both made peace with my fear and clarified my intentions, my work slowly shifted from a local to a national and later to an international stage and from smaller, local entrepreneurs to multinational firms and even foreign governments.

I am sure that the rock ledge and waterfall are not completely responsible, but I am not sure that I would have had the courage to take on the new challenges before. In my old fear trance, I would be more likely to respond, "I don't work with large companies," or "I work only with entrepreneurs," or "I just work in this region."

Since learning to listen to my internal guidance system, to use my fear as a tool that gives me information and then to move toward it, I regularly do things now that friends seem to think take great courage. When I think about where I was a few years ago, I guess they're right, but I hardly even think about it now. Fear never does go away because it is a healthy part of change given to us or evolved in us to help us learn where to be careful and what to give attention so we will be able to survive. It isn't intended to stop us. When we become accustomed to moving toward our fears, doing so becomes easier and easier, and things that once frightened us terribly may hardly raise a reaction from us at all later.

At one time in each of our lives, reporting to our first responsible job was quite frightening. Now most of us go to work regularly with hardly a thought. Only because we were not willing to let our fear stop us have we reached the place where it no longer bothers us at all.

Chaos Can Be Frightening

Because most of the companies in which I work are fast-growth, entrepreneurial companies, it often feels to the people in them like they are working in the middle of a hurricane. Change is constant and intense, and to call conditions chaotic is in no way an over-statement. It is not uncommon in this country for such promising companies to die of what appears to be implosion. The energy that created the company was not able to make the transition to orderly operations without killing the creativity that gave it promise in the first place. People that work in these companies know that the odds for long-term employment are not good, and the owners know that as well. It is not at all uncommon for people to express to me their fears that the organization will die. When a company has grown from 5 or 10 employees to 150 or 200 in two years, the owner often carries a significant self-assumed burden of responsi-bility "for all those people out there and their families who are depending on their paychecks."

I encourage both the owners and their employees to talk about their fears and use them to learn. Saying the words "I'm afraid . . ." brings about instant bonding and purposefulness. When others join in and say "I'm afraid of that, too," we have laid the groundwork for using those fears as a source of learning and for determining what actions are needed to prevent the fears from becoming reality. A vigorous learning session often leaves people knowing exactly what each must do to prevent what they fear, *and* maybe even more important, they leave feeling that each person *can* do something, rather than just be scared.

I have seen a company choose to put a major growth initia-tive on hold when they discovered that, if they did what they had planned, they wouldn't be able to deliver on the new busi-ness that was generated, resulting in unhappy customers and bad publicity. In this case and many similar ones, people actually heaved a sigh of relief, because everyone had known intuitively it wouldn't work, but everyone had been *afraid* to say the words. When the words were said, the company and the individuals in it regained their power to make meaningful change.

This is what emotional competence looks like at work. Peo-ple honor their feelings as important data, and they talk about them with each other. When decisions are made in emotionally competent organizations, emotional data is treated as seriously as market studies, cost-benefit analysis and return-on-investment studies. We don't choose one or the other, all are considered sources of critical data.

In *Descartes' Error: Emotion, Reason, and the Human Brain*, Antonio Damasio, chairman of the neurology department for the University of Iowa College of Medicine, demonstrates "that decisions based solely on rational reflection without the participation of emotional elements lead to bad consequences. In other words, your feelings can help you do the right thing."[6]

Without emotional competence, people let their fear of speaking up or their fear of hearing what they don't want to hear stifle important decision-making information.

Organizations are systems of human beings. When we as human beings learn emotional competence in our workplaces and in our lives, we can be more alive, at work, at home, in our communities, and in our organizations. Our organizations never will be healthy, either experientially or competitively, as long as they are composed of emotional zombies. Our lives and our organizations are robbed of depth, variety, learning, and richness when we choose to live in trances. Emotional competence will allow us to come alive personally and organizationally.

Transforming the Fear

- On a deeper level, many of us resist waking up because, when we are sleepwalking, we aren't responsible. Many of us are stuck in our suffering as victims. We cannot get on with our lives until we forgive and stop being victims. When we regain our inner power, we have more accountability, less blaming, and we stop being victims.
- Emotional competence requires that we abandon being motivated by external judgments and shift to listening to our Higher Self to decide how to act in life.
- As we grow, each transition point will require us to give up part of who we may have thought we were. Each time we do

that, some people in our life system will be upset because they want us to remain who we have been (who they want us to be) rather than who we really are. When we are awake, we are going against what the dominant culture says we should be, which is asleep.

- Although we often struggle for long periods at each transition point, the moment we have courage to give voice to our intentions, everything changes. We no longer struggle with *whether* to do what we know is right; the question becomes *how* to do what we know we must do.
- Forgiveness is critical to leaving the past behind and living in the present.
- Facing fear in any area of our lives gives us courage for facing fear in other areas.
- The chaos of rapid growth and change is frightening. Whenever groups talk together about their fears, they regain their power to make meaningful change, which brings order to the chaos. When we make decisions based simply on rational data, we overlook significant, important data.

Chaos and the Fear of Not-Knowing

"We are talking about products that are still evolving, delivered to a market that is still emerging, via a technology that is still changing on a daily basis."

. . . KENT FOSTER,
senor executive at GTE[1]

"This place is complete chaos. You've never seen anything like this!" Keith is an executive at a company that has grown from 20 employees to 400 in about 18 months. New employees are hired and report to work, but there's nowhere to put them—no desk, no phone, no office space—and no one knows what they are supposed to do. At the same time, the rest of the employees are working horrendously long hours just to keep their heads above water but increasingly feel like drowning is imminent.

Customer service telephone lines are continually busy, with a large bank of calls always on hold. This is largely due to orders that frequently are up to six weeks late and of poor quality. Exhausted employees move product through to fill late orders without much attention to how they are working. The returned merchandise room is overflowing.

Costs associated with processing defective orders that have been returned have escalated the cost-per-unit dramatically. Capital investment needs have jumped as the company responds to increased order volume with new equipment, plant, and office space. Cash flow is so tight that a bank note sometimes is required to meet the payroll.

"We've got to get things under control here, or we're out of business," Keith says, "We've got to stop this chaos."

I ask Keith what he suggests they do. "We've got to watch the cost per unit and bring it back into our target range, and we've got to get more out of these people. They just don't care. They don't produce as much as I know they could, and they don't seem to care about what they do produce."

I ask Keith if the company has been tracking the cost per unit, and he responds with a bar graph that shows daily cost per piece over three months. He is right: this measure has been rising steadily. I ask him what else the company has been doing, and he reports that it has done three things. First, managers discuss the problem at every meeting. Second, each manager is supposed to talk to those under his or her direction and get them to reduce scrap materials. Finally, he says, they have done a publicity blitz in the company, with posters and paycheck stuffers about cutting costs.

"How long have you been doing those things?" I ask him. He reports that it started about four months ago, when costs seemed to rise dramatically. "Has it made any difference?" I asked. In the beginning, he says, it improved a little bit, but then seemed to return to the general pattern.

My meeting with Keith is not unlike many that I have had with clients and potential clients, many of whom start our meetings describing some form of chaos reigning in their company. The catalyst for the chaos may come from a number of sources, from new competition entering a market or new technology that threatens the demand for a product at one extreme to "too much of a good thing" on the other.

Too much of a good thing usually happens when an advertisement in a national publication produces orders far in excess of the company's capacity or when marketing lands the "really big one"—the account that everyone has dreamed of getting, without dreaming about how the company would satisfy the Big Guy's requirements. Occasionally, the company has identified a real hole in the market and the natural demand is far in excess of what the start-up operation can meet. The sales department is paid on the number of orders taken, and so they make promises that production doesn't know about and couldn't possibly deliver.

Whatever the source of the chaos, the response almost always is the same. One or two indicators are identified and tracked. People talk about them a lot. Much discussion focuses on control and getting more out of people. Employees don't understand why they have to work such long hours for minimal pay when they obviously have so much business. There must be money to hire more people and pay better. Morale usually is low because, despite the hard work, employees keep getting lectures. The managers are fit to be tied: they've tried everything they know and can't seem to control costs. At the same time, they know that they cannot continue to produce poor-quality products, make late deliveries, and expect to stay in business.

Chaos occurs when a system becomes "utterly unpredictable."[1] By definition, *chaos* is a "state . . . of total confusion or disorder."[2] Even though we are admitting, just by use of the word, that chaos is unpredictable and disordered, invariably managers respond to chaos by wanting control. They become linear, analytical, and focused on key measures or processes. They attempt to produce an orderly result in an environment that, by definition, is so unpredictable that it cannot be analyzed. It doesn't work. So, what do they do? More of the same—seek control to no avail. By the time I arrive, they are bloodied, bruised, frustrated, exasperated, exhausted, and still grasping desperately for control of the chaos.

The Nature of Chaos

This picture came to mind as I stood watching the hurricane from my bedroom window at 2 a.m. For managers to seek control in the midst of organizational chaos is as futile as if I insisted on serving a picnic lunch on the patio in the middle of that storm, trying to control my environment to make it happen.

Most conventional management training or even conventional thinking has told us that we should control the system, control the workers, control key measures, and control the results. That is the trance from which most of us work, day in and day out. This approach works only in the most ordered of work environments and only minimally well then, because it stifles creativity, growth, and development—all of which are naturally messy, disordered, and chaotic. For most of us, however, it is the only trance we know, so we insist on sticking to it, even to the point of being totally depleted of our natural human energy for the creative process. This is supposed to work; it may even have worked before at some point. We're afraid to try anything else. We've been led to believe that nothing else works. The response to try to get control is a trance, but in chaos, almost anything works better than a trance. Chaos requires us to be fully awake and observant, eagerly and actively gathering information about conditions in our environment.

Continual Cocreation in Community

Whether we call it chaos or just rapid change, hardly an organization in existence can survive working in the same routine manner every day over a sustained period of time. Flexibility, resilience, openness, and adaptability are the watchwords of 21st century workplaces. All of them require that we give up our routine, our working in trances, and enter a new state.

The new state is the state of continual cocreation in community. Continual cocreation in community is not the product of strategic planning sessions, during which a select group of individuals who have anointed themselves with ultimate wisdom for the enterprise sit in a room and decide what it should do and how it should do it. Continual cocreation in community involves the whole system, including employees, customers, and suppliers, in an ongoing creative process. It is chaotic. It emerges day by day, sometimes hour by hour, through an open flow of information, open and respectful relationships, and a common sense of purpose.

Purposeful cocreation occurs when all the people in the system (those in the company at all levels, as well as those with whom they interact in the marketplace) have a clear and personal sense about what they are in business to do. (Although I say "in business," this really applies to the express reason for existence of any organization, be it public, private, or nonprofit.) If we say we want to offer leading-edge widget products and services by listening and being responsive to customers' needs, every single person in the organization knows what that means to him or her personally. We know that customers include the folks in the next department and marketing and collections as well as the people who take our widgets home and use them. We know how to listen. We know what it means to be responsive, and we are free to exercise whatever discretion is necessary to be responsive.

Often our organizations suffer from "multiple personality disorders" or "organizational schizophrenia."[3] There are so many rules that people are afraid to do or say anything. Rules contradict one another, and more important, they often contradict the expressed purpose of the firm. For purposeful cocreation to occur, there must be no mixed messages from management about listening to customers and then failing to listen to employees. We don't tell our employees to be responsive to customers and then punish them when they break a "rule" to do so. Everyone knows that the rules we have are there for one purpose—to allow us to listen and be responsive to the customers. The result is a lot fewer rules. We all have a sense of common purpose.

In continual cocreation, we engage with each other about how we can accomplish more fully what is a clear and shared sense of purpose. Everyone in the organization has a role in the cocreation of its realization. A free flow of information is essential for continual cocreation, because each of the members of the organization carries within his or her mind a piece of the evolving creation. No parts are unimportant or expendable—every person is essential to the process. This moves beyond a trendy teamwork schema to a whole new way of communication. Despite the need for more and better group process and decision making brought about by encouraging more participation, most companies continue to rely on the same communication and decision-making tools they used when working and making decisions as individuals. The consequence is a phenomena I call *inverse intelligence*.

One would expect that, when a group of bright people come together to make a decision or analyze a problem, their combined abilities would result in a group intelligence greater than that of any individual. Instead, most groups experience exactly the opposite—inverse intelligence. The resulting group intelligence is significantly less than that of any of the individuals within it. In simple terms, if the average intelligence of the individuals in a group is 120, the group intelligence will often be 60 or 70, rather than 150.

For example, let's look at the group, mentioned at the beginning of this book, that got together to discuss the process of implementing new technology. They failed to exercise even the normal individual intelligence because of fear. Each was afraid that he or she would be the only manager who didn't support the proposed schedule, yet each one had reservations. The decision enacted from inverse intelligence led to a near disaster because no one was willing or brave enough to share the unique view of the operation and transition that each held.

Any one of the participants could have improved the quality of the decision, but instead, they were afraid to exercise even the judgment that normal individual intelligence would have dictated. The group made a decision that reflected a group intelligence much lower than that of individuals who composed it.

Cocreation requires a group of individuals to learn to think together, so they may discover things as a group that would not have been possible outside of the group setting. This approach demands a free flow of information. It requires asking dozens and dozens of questions and generating more and more information. Information is the food of cocreation: recognizing and talking about what we are feeling, when we are afraid, and learning to use our emotions, our hopes, and our dreams are important components of the group learning process.

Whenever I am involved in assembling people from throughout an organization to engage in inquiry, in at least one (and often several) incidences, people from different parts of the organization discover that they have been working on the same problem in isolation. When the information begins to flow, they often discover that, although they have been working on the same problem, they view it from different perspectives. When the parties begin sharing information, the creative energy explodes. Often individuals in other parts of the enterprise will add other pieces, and before the day is out, progress that would never have occurred in isolation has begun, often moving a solution beyond problem solving to experimentation and even implementation. This is cocreation, and it occurs naturally when information flows openly.

Giving Up the Trances

Cocreation in community means that week by week, day by day, and even hour by hour, we work together in a state I call *not-*

knowing. The state occurs because we are willing to embrace the unpredictability of chaos instead of resisting it. We give up what our trance states have told us we "should" do. We give up what our trance states have told us to expect. We give up what our trance states have told us we should want. And, we embrace the fact that we do not know what to do, what to expect, and what we want. In the group process discussed in the preceding section, if each of the individuals working on the same problem in different departments came together with the belief that he or she had the answer, information would not and could not have flowed, and quantum leaps in idea development would have been lost. The collective intelligence could not have grown.

When we cocreate, we hold ourselves open to a rich flow of information and dialogue in emptiness—empty of knowing what the answers are or even how to go about getting the answers, and in the process, we become vulnerable to truth. To be vulnerable to the truth, we must empty ourselves of what I think or what you think and make ourselves available to a higher standard of truth that embraces the wisdom of paradox and the unknown. Some call this place *complexity*. Some call it *confusion* or *emptiness*. I like *not-knowing*, because it says exactly the state in which we must be.

Whatever it is called, it is the place where chaos and order overlap. It is the leading edge. It is dynamic and ever changing. And, we can get there only by not-knowing. The minute even one of us brings an idea to the table to which he or she knows the right answer or the right course of action, analysis of the concept that has been put forth will distract the group from the wisdom of its collective learning. Whether we are in chaos and wanting to move toward order or stuck in a totally ordered environment sucked dry of creativity and innovation, if we collectively hold ourselves in a state of mind that is not-knowing, ask lots of curious questions, and start information flowing, our native creativity will move us to the dynamic leading edge where order and chaos coexist.

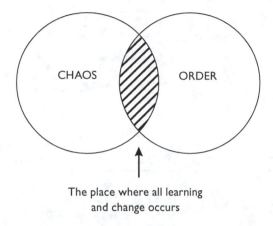

The place where all learning
and change occurs

Figure 5-1   *Relationship of Chaos and Order*

The Place of Not-Knowing

The universe of possibilities has four different ways of knowing. Some things we know we know, and some things we know that we don't know. For instance, I know my name, where I was born, and where I live. I am quite certain about these. I also am certain about some things that I don't know about. I know nothing about microbiology or what it is like to live in a country at war. Our trances are designed to help us survive in a world where everything is as we believe it is. They foster the illusion that we know how things are and that everything is totally clear and predictable. There are no ifs, ands, and buts—things just are. We know what is right and what the facts are. It is a very black-and-white world.

As much as our trances would like us to believe that's all there is, a much larger part of our universe is composed of what we don't know. Again, there are two possibilities. First, there are things that we think we don't know that we actually do know. For instance, a few years ago I thought I knew nothing about quantum physics. Then I read a book explaining organizational behavior in terms of quantum physics, and I discovered I really

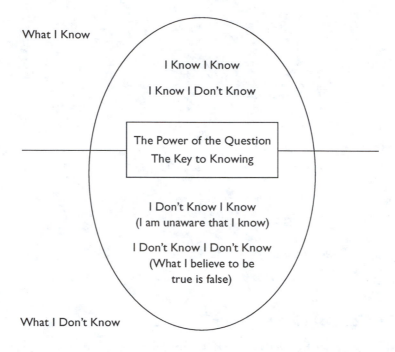

What I Know

I Know I Know

I Know I Don't Know

The Power of the Question
The Key to Knowing

I Don't Know I Know
(I am unaware that I know)

I Don't Know I Don't Know
(What I believe to be
true is false)

What I Don't Know

Figure 5-2   *Ways of Knowing*

knew quite a bit about the subject. I just hadn't known it was quantum physics. All of us have things that we know that we aren't aware of knowing.

It is quite common in my work to have someone say to me, "I don't know." I can never resist asking the individual, "If you did know, what would you know?" And, almost without fail, they begin telling me much more about the subject that just a few seconds earlier they had told me they "didn't know" about. Usually, within less than five minutes, the person is quite clear about the subject. The person really knew, but was living in a trance in which he or she believed they didn't know. When I use a few questions to bring people like this into present time and then consciously into not-knowing, they come to know what "they didn't know" they knew.

A second set of possibilities about what we don't know comprises things that we don't know we don't know: this is what we believe to be true that actually is false. We think we know, but we just don't know that we don't know. In Keith's company, and many like it, managers believe that the way out of chaos is through control. Trying to control chaos will bring only more chaos, along with high levels of frustration and stress. The managers believe they have the answer, but they don't know they don't know. They don't know what they believe to be true is actually false.

These two sets of possibilities constitute the domain of not-knowing. When we can hold ourselves in this place long enough, either individually or collectively, making ourselves vulnerable to the truth through personal or collective questioning, we will learn something new—always.

Not-knowing is an uncomfortable place. It requires us to be wide awake. It requires our trances to surrender to conscious open inquiry and the tension that comes from not-knowing in a world that believes we must know. And, it requires questions.

The Power of the Question

Questions invite a higher standard of truth. They help us individually and collectively to discover what we know that we didn't know we knew and what we didn't know that we didn't know. Unless a wake-up call jars our reality, most of us won't choose to doubt that our "stories" are the truth. One of my favorite questions to ask teams of managers who believe they know how things are is, "What if the opposite were true?" To their astonishment, further exploration often demonstrates that some part of the opposite actually *is* true. They just didn't know.

The conscious mind has the capacity to process seven pieces of information per minute. The unconscious mind can process 300,000 pieces in the same amount of time. The nonlinear, nonverbal right brain has 50 times more brain cells than the overused left brain, on which our organizations have become so totally dependent. Most of this vast library of information is carried around in our not-knowing. It is the storehouse that, when questioned, clears the mirrors of awareness and enables a more accurate assessment of "where we are," both individually and collectively, so that conscious movement can begin toward creating what we choose to create.

The power to move us to this new knowing that comes from our not-knowing lies in questions—open-ended, curious, naive questions. Open and curious inquiry allows us to play with ideas we might never have considered before. It helps us become aware of what we have assumed to be true that was false and what "facts" really are just beliefs. It helps us discover how many of our habits and practices have grown out of our trances, because ultimately the power of the question is that it demands we leave our trances behind. The power of the question demands that we wake up long enough to search our cerebral and intuitive data banks and discover something new. It demands that we let go of entrenched beliefs motivated by fear-induced protectionism and speak from our inner truth and innocence.

Discussion is our most common way of communicating in organizations. I share my ideas about how things are; then others share theirs. After that, each of us tries to wear down the others by convincing them that our ideas are the best. This kind of communication is fear and trance generated, and it breeds inverse intelligence.

To make collective intelligence more accessible, we need to engage in group learning, using dialogue. The word *dialogue* suggests learning across a group rather than within ourselves, and really effective dialogue depends much more on having the right questions than on having the right answers. It depends on the willingness of participants to acknowledge that individually they don't know. Groups using dialogue seek to develop a deep understanding of all sides of an issue, flooding themselves with information until a solution emerges. They begin building the collective intelligence of the group.

Instead of presenting positions that are defended, individuals holding themselves in not-knowing seek to expand the inquiry by asking more and deeper questions. The result is that links, implications, complexities, and impediments surface that are often overlooked in traditional decision-making discussions. It has been my experience that individuals actually come to be of one mind as the concerns and perspectives of each person are explored. This is *not* consensus building, a process by which people artificially press others toward a single position on which all agree. When we forsake the goal of a single position we can agree on and we hold ourselves collectively in not-knowing, we come to be of one mind. It seems that we truly can come to be of one mind only by giving that up as a goal.

An environment in which we are awake, aware of what our fears are, including our fear of not-knowing the answer and the fear of being held in not-knowing, is critical to building this kind of collective intelligence. This is the only way in which we can improve the quality of both our decisions and the process by which those decisions are made.

Building Collective Intelligence

Over a three-month period, I was involved in a process that consciously took a large group of people from two departments into not-knowing and held them there while we built the collective intelligence. The process was introduced after a small war broke out between the departments over which one should be responsible for a rather onerous but important monthly function. One could have made a case for either department performing the task, but it was a no-win situation. Whichever department would have gotten "stuck" with the work would have screamed "injustice," and although a decision may have been made, the war would have only accelerated.

Using the company's electronic mail system, we created intentional chaos; our goal was to confuse people that were quite certain that they had the right answer. We wanted to take them into their not-knowing and hold them there long enough to discover new possibilities. We asked them lots of questions, and we asked them to generate open-ended questions about the process. We even asked them to design experiments to test any assumptions we might be making. We invited people in other departments to participate, both electronically and, when we finally got together, in face-to-face group learning. Not many did, but a few contributed ideas that challenged the certainties of those who were more immediately involved in the process.

After two months, we invited anyone in the company who was interested to join us for group learning. Several pages of questions and data generated by the various experiments we had conducted were distributed in advance, so when we came into the room, participants were overwhelmed with information—frustrated, too. In a culture so bent on believing we have the answers, there is little patience for learning. We generally just want an answer, even if it is the wrong one. If we had polled people coming into the room that morning, we would have gotten a variety of what they believed to be "obvious answers," all of which would have been wrong.

At the end of about five hours of data sharing, asking questions, sending for more data, and mapping the flow of a customer through the whole system, it became clear to everyone that the function provoking the war wasn't even the problem—it was a symptom of a problem that occurred much earlier in the customer flow. As the group slowly came to be of one mind, it was apparent that it would take at least six months to catch up on the backlog of problems producing the symptom, but it could be done. A number of suggestions surfaced for facilitating the transition period, and members of *both* departments *volunteered* to assist the other and work as a team to ease the change.

The result of the sustained chaos and not-knowing was a resolution that left people feeling satisfied we were on the right track, didn't blame anyone, energized people to assist in the implementation, and genuinely addressed the problem, not just the symptom. Any solution that would have been proposed earlier in the process would have addressed the symptom. Our group learning demonstrated that any solution aimed at the symptom would have resulted only in a continued mushrooming of the problem the company had experienced in the preceding year.

When we have the courage and patience to consciously and collectively go and stay in not-knowing, we make ourselves vulnerable to group learning, an increased collective intelligence, and a higher standard of the truth.

Not-Knowing Opens Us to Self-Organization

In recent years, increasing interest by those who study organizations has examined what have been called *self-organizing systems*.[4] Researchers have been discovering that human systems, such as those in our organizations, are similar to those occurring everywhere in nature. They share the incredible capacity to re-create themselves with no external direction when they have a clear sense of self-identity, an understanding of the human and process relationships in the system, and a free flow of information to tell them what is needed. They need no boss to tell them what to do. If the conditions are right, the group will always find the best answer for what needs to be done. In the group process I previously described, three managers did participate, but as equals with all others. In actuality, I believe the process was something of an amazement to them. They spent much of the time in wide-eyed observation listening to the energetic participation and input of the department members.

The most easily recognizable example of how self-organizational activity emerges occurs during a disaster.[5] People just naturally figure out what needs to be done, and then they do it. No one tells them. No one analyzes and directs. It just happens. Following my recent hurricane experience, examples of this kind of self-organization were everywhere. A woman who had a camera and film walked through the neighborhood taking pictures for people to use in filing their insurance claims so that they could begin repairing damage. A man with a chain saw cut up fallen trees blocking the street, and others jumped in to help move the wood out of the way. One woman who had grown up with hurricanes and kept a case of candles on hand gave them to neighbors and friends, many of whom would be without electricity for up to two weeks. The family that had thought to fill the bathtub before the water supply was contaminated offered pitchers of clean water to those without it. Even the grocery store trucked in semitrailers of ice to give away to those without refrigeration in the sweltering heat that followed the storm. No one was standing around figuring out who should do what and then giving orders—people just seemed to know what to do. They self-organized.

This process happens naturally and easily, if we let it. What gets in the way are the individuals and groups that feel like somebody *should* figure it out and give orders. This implies that some*one* knows. Some*one* can never know what the best action is. It can be known only when we come together in not-knowing to share our respective information and perspectives and then self-organize. Only by not-knowing are we able to build the collective intelligence to allow self-organization to occur.

Whether we exist in a temporarily ordered world or a chaotic one, when we ask enough curious questions from not-knowing, we will move ourselves to the dynamic edge where chaos and order overlap—the place where meaningful change occurs naturally, the place where we remember how to self-organize. When we stop assuming and begin asking, we open ourselves to new knowledge. But, this can happen only from not-knowing.

This need for not-knowing—questioning what we do know and opening ourselves to the chaos of self-organization—presents a serious concern from the perspective of transforming fear. In almost every group with which I've worked, at least one (sometimes more) individual is the "know-it-all." He or she can cite studies and sources and often speak eloquently, if somewhat pretentiously, about the obvious course of action. This individual has learned to survive by regularly putting on the "expert" trance. These people will stridently resist any efforts toward building group intelligence that demand a position of not-knowing. This requires that the individual forsake his or her most reliable survival mechanism and go into a metaphoric free-fall into not-knowing. It is critical to work with these individuals around their fear of not-knowing, because their pontificating regularly shuts down the meaningful dialogue of cocreation in a community.

The minute anyone of us *believes* we know, the process will stop. The minute anyone of us *believes* we know, others will be afraid to speak because they will be afraid they don't have the "right" answer; they will be afraid of looking foolish. People begin to wear themselves down just trying to resist natural tendencies to discover and create, eventually giving in to the person who thinks he or she has the answer.

This is the essential function that chaos plays in stimulating learning. Because, by definition, conditions are totally unpredictable, chaos confuses us about what reality is. By so doing, it helps us "unlearn" what we have believed to be true, allowing us to open to new possibilities. The nature of chaos takes us into our not-knowing.

Be it a group of two or a companywide problem-solving initiative such as the one described earlier in this chapter, when a group is willing to hold itself in not-knowing long enough, new possibilities emerge. Simultaneously, an incredible aliveness, enthusiasm, and energy results as individuals come together to become a creative new entity, they come to be part of something bigger than themselves.

One executive was being very intentional about creating a culture in which he and members of his division held themselves in not-knowing so that they could learn together. The executive reported that he and one of his managers sustained the not-knowing for almost two months on a particular topic. He said that, ordinarily, they would have just made a decision in the first session, but they wanted to do it differently this time. With delight in his eyes and voice, he told the story in the manager's presence. He revealed how they had come up with a solution that was far more creative, effective, and satisfying to all involved. The manager who had hung in there with him for the two months agreed heartily. This is what continual cocreation in a community is about, and it demands that we embrace the fear of not-knowing and develop the courage to sustain the ambiguity long enough for the "more creative, effective, and satisfying" solution to emerge.

Accepting Our Fears and Staying with Them

Self-organization and free flow of information and their companion concepts of letting go of control, gatekeeping, agendas, privileged information, planning, and goals are frightening to many. Although we may not say so, our actions in organizations demonstrate that generally we have feared the free flow of information and the chaos we believe the information creates. We have been afraid information might get into the "wrong" hands. Once it got into the wrong hands, people would begin asking questions and challenging the status quo, which might lead to self-organization around new ideas. This, in turn, might lead to chaos for those who are invested in maintaining the way things have been. We have restricted the agenda, fearing that something might be discussed before conditions were "right" or controlled to produce the outcome we wanted, implying that people might organize themselves around a different approach. We fear that, if information really flowed, something might come out that would make one or more of us "look bad."

What others think about us is a major concern to most people. We don't want to "look bad." Consequently, we would rather take less effective action and produce mediocre results than risk "going for the gold" and failing. Human development consultant and speaker Jean Houston has said, "I find that for most people 90 percent of their energies are bound up wondering what the other person is going to think."⁶ When "looking good" is a higher priority than making a good decision for most of us, it doesn't take much imagination to figure out why our organizations operate far below optimum.

Rather than embracing chaos and self-organization, which always will organize itself in the most effective way, our organizations are riddled with those who fear exactly that.

Our demands for predictability have become the insurance of mediocrity. They have ensured "some" result, even if it wasn't the best, the most creative, or what any of us really wanted; and we could promise that we would deliver it most of the time. And, until the last couple of decades, most of the time we could promise to deliver it without chaos. Those who are risk averse would rather cling to mediocrity than risk greatness, with its accompanying potential risk for unexpected results.

The trances that produce the predictability of mediocrity sound high-minded and committed to the good of the organization, but they produce just the opposite. Our fear trance that wants to know, coupled with our fear trance that requires predictability, lead us to evoke the excuse of not wasting time or saving time. A guilt trance leads us to quit the process before we generate enough information to build the collective intelligence to the point where we can self-organize in a new way.

Our trance that thinks we must be perfect sucks us out of present time, even though the only meaningful information is about the present and is available only when we are in present time. What happened in the past is finished, and the future is not yet here. We must be vigilant to keep ourselves totally present and in present time to sustain not-knowing. If we drift to another time and place, we tend to begin to believe that we "know," but what we will know will inevitably be about something in the past or the future, not about what conditions exist and what we know at this moment.

Choosing Not-Knowing

We have two choices about getting to not-knowing: we can resist chaos until, stressed out, bloodied, and bruised, we are dragged from the trance of what we believed we knew; or we can consciously and voluntarily choose to go there. Both personal and organizational history has been that most of us go to not-knowing only when forced. Consequently, it hasn't been a pleasant place to be, and most choose to stay there only long enough to get enough information for a quick fix that will take them out of the immediate pain as quickly as possible.

Given the history that most people go to not-knowing only through the bloodied and bruised route, consciously choosing to hold ourselves in not-knowing not only fails to hold appeal but actually is frightening. What is wonderful about the conscious choice route is that we can skip the pain up front. As we have more and more experiences with the energy, enthusiasm, and joy that come from building the collective intelligence to the point of self-organization, we actually can grow to embrace the process.

Even if we consciously choose to enter not-knowing and expect positive outcomes, we always will face fear in the process. This is where emotional competence becomes so important. At any time in not-knowing when we encounter information that causes us to give up a belief about how the world is, we most likely will slip into another fear trance, related to that belief and all of the habits we have nurtured to support it. When we move from knowing to not-knowing, in some small way, we must give up the world as we have known it. That process may occur once or twice or it may occur a dozen times in a given process. But, whenever we slip into our trances, we leave present time, and we stop being vigilant in gathering information about changing conditions, which we can influence right now.

Emotional competence is about feeling what we are feeling in present time and accepting that in ourselves and in others. It supports us in sustaining not-knowing because we are conscious of our own tendencies to slip into trances and those of others to do the same. Instead of having a lot of entranced people bumping against each other's trances, all of which are grasping for knowing, we can be fully awake and sustain not-knowing. When we are awake, we can use the information our emotions provide us to enhance our collective intelligence.

So, for instance, in the process of mining not-knowing, we may come up against information telling us that we may have to do something we haven't done in the past. Our trance state is likely to begin searching for what sounds like reasons why this approach won't work. The purpose of searching what we believe we know to find a reason why something new won't work is to protect us. If our protective fear mechanisms can come up with a "reason" for not trying something new that sounds rational, then we won't be required to do something new at which we may fail and lose our job. The trance reactions sound like, "Do we have budget for that?" "Can we do that with our current staff?" "Will that violate our policy?" and other reactions that indicate a knowing position. The fear that produces the trance state is really about failing and losing our jobs, not about whether the new approach will work or not. If we lack the emotional competence to recognize when we are slipping into our trances, that distinction will be lost on us.

If we have the emotional competence to recognize this difference, then we can continue to function in current time. We can ask our fears what additional information we need in order to move toward them. We can then say, "I've never done anything like that before. What would it entail? Is training available? Has someone in this group done something like it before, someone who would assist me or coach me?" All these questions are about learning in the present, not reacting from a trance out of fear of losing one's job. They are not-knowing questions that add to the growing collective intelligence and help us learn together about being more effective.

When we go for the quick fix, the easy solution, or the surface answer, we may experience a quick high followed by a never-ending series of new problems that wear us down and send us again and again seeking yet one more quick fix with its quick high. We become problem-solving addicts, always seeking the high of the quick fix, even when we know the inevitability of the low that unfailingly follows.

When our organizations choose question marks, contemplation, being present, and not-knowing, we face our fears, fear of not having the answer, fear of not looking brilliantly analytical, fear of "wasting time" on an emotional process, and fear of silence.

A team that throws itself into not-knowing and consciously holds itself there, at "the point before becoming this or that," will discover its own magic—the magic of collective intelligence, the magic of being able to consciously choose what it will cocreate rather than endlessly taking the quick fix, easy response, and long-term downward spiral of despair.

I already have spoken about the small manufacturing company making an 18-month transition from top-down, owner-generated decision making about almost everything to a team's ever-evolving collective intelligence dynamically driving the company. It started with doubt and fear. The owner was afraid the team couldn't do it. The team was afraid the owner couldn't let go and would fire one or more of them if they made a wrong decision.

In the beginning, both sides had to test the waters. Changing the corporate culture required each person to know what he or she must do to transcend the habits of the current culture and the trance states in which all had operated: trance states that caused the owner to always want to jump in and fix it; trance states that said, "It won't work here. We're not smart enough!"; trance states in which employees always shrugged their shoulders and said "I don't know," without even taking time to think about whether they might know anything that would help; trance states that said "We're behind in production; we don't have time to talk." Each trance state was based in fear and helped keep everyone locked into a company culture that no one liked any more. They had to consciously choose to be awake and transcend each habitual trance (see box).

Trance	Associated Fears
"It'll be a disaster if *I* don't fix it."	Not so subtle: Fear of mistakes, loss of money or reputation
	Subtle: Fear that others might solve the problem better; I won't be needed
"It won't work here. They're not smart enough."	Not so subtle: Fear of mistakes, loss of money or reputation
	Subtle: Fear that others might solve the problem better; I won't be needed
"It won't work here. We're not smart enough."	Not so subtle: Fear of mistakes, loss of job, family security, and the like
	Subtle: Fear of ability to survive; fear of power and responsibility if I discover I am smart enough
"I don't know."	Not so subtle: Fear of mistakes, loss of job, family security, and the like
	Subtle: Fear of ability to survive; fear of power and responsibility if I discover I am smart enough
"We don't have time to talk."	Not so subtle: If we take time to talk, someone might discover I don't have the answer; I won't meet production deadlines, might lose customers, might lose job and family security, might have to work overtime
	Subtle: Fear of ability to survive; fear of power and responsibility if I discover I am smart enough
"I don't make a difference."	Not so subtle: I'm afraid to stick my neck out (or stick it out again); I'm afraid things will never change; I'm afraid I'll get in trouble
	Subtle: Fear of power and responsibility if I discover I can start dramatic change by myself; I'm afraid I'll get something started and won't be able to sustain it

First came a shipping problem. Then a conflict arose that needed to be resolved. Later came some performance issues. Each time, the owner knew he had to transcend his habit of believing *he* had the answers, and with trepidation, the team gingerly walked into not-knowing, asking questions, and learning to hold themselves open to new learning. Each time it was frightening. Each time it was stressful as they transcended the attraction to a quick fix. Each time the process ended with a better solution than any*one* could have generated. Sometimes the solutions were especially tough because the employees had to look at uncomfortable issues and face their personal fears of saying or doing something that another "wouldn't like."

The team still is learning, but after about a year, the owner noticed that people had stopped coming to him for answers because they had learned he would give them no answers, only questions. They have discovered their collective intelligence, and they have learned how to cocreate in a community with only occasional input from the boss.

This team and others who are having the courage to learn to be with not-knowing discover a magic much more fulfilling than the high of the quick fix with its inevitable "hangover." They discover the joy of new knowing, the synergy of collective intelligence, and the energy, enthusiasm, and joy of entering together into a creative space where individuals cannot go.

Resist the Future or Allow It

The nature of 21st century organizations and the nature of 21st century life will be that of "not knowing." Despite all of our efforts to the contrary, we can know little about the future with any certainty. We may have faith in certain people, who will never let us down, but we have no way of knowing that those people will be alive next week or next month or even an hour from now. It probably always has been that way, but the rapid pace of change in our world makes us more keenly aware of how much is changing and how it is affecting each of us.

For most of us in traditional Western culture, this kind of uncertainty and continuous change produces fear. When we have not developed the emotional competence to make peace with our fears, we fight the inevitable. Our trance-induced, fear-driven actions pursue options perceived as safe, when safety always is an illusion, and seek to control the future, a futile exercise at best. Our inability to consciously accept our fears and learn from them drives us to look for quick fixes and easy, short-term solutions, which take us out of our pain but rob us of the richness and internal power that come from sustaining the not-knowing or emptiness.

Conversely, when we choose to know and experience our emotions, being with the confusion and agony of not-knowing, we inevitably emerge with a renewed vigor for life—a new aliveness, rich with possibility. Our courage allows us to create new options, to try things we haven't tried before, and to learn to think together in community with others so that we can learn to think things we've never thought before. We see and embrace more and more opportunities. We still have our fears, but we move toward them rather than let them lull us back into a reactive trance state.

All change occurs in the place of not-knowing. We are capable of learning new ways only when we are willing to give up the old ways. The old way would be to jump in there and press, try to control, or try to convert or convince another that what we have known in the past is what dictates the present. When we are in not-knowing, we don't know what we don't know. We don't know that what we may be trying to teach, to control, and to press for is suited only for a world that no longer exists. If we are to forge into a new world, we can do so only from a place of learning, from a place of not-knowing, from a place of surrender. That is where we can adopt the "beginner's mind," the stance of the naive inquirer, and ask curious questions—the very questions that lead us to new knowledge.

The ego is the part that believes it knows. When we are able to put aside our egos and give up believing that we know, we make space for our wise inner knowledge to emerge in the space created by our not-knowing.

Not-knowing is a place of complete ambiguity, of paradox and contradictions. To stay in our place of not-knowing long enough for our inner wisdom to emerge requires that we immerse ourselves in confusion and not-knowing. We must forsake the ego, looking brilliantly analytical and clever, and having the answers. We must consciously surrender to the not-knowing. It requires us to be awake and mindful of what we are feeling so that we can use that as data for learning. It requires discipline and practice. It requires that we consciously, blissfully, and without apology say, "I do not know. I cannot know alone." We can come to new wisdom only by leaving our individual and collective egos behind and moving together into the not-knowing.

The uneasiness of the chaos that occurs as we generate more and more information can tempt us to move back to what we believed we knew or to where we feel like we're "making progress" or "getting somewhere." It could have happened with the group process during which we took several months to ask questions, do experiments, and gather data. It could have happened during the ongoing sustenance of ambiguity between the executive and the manager who waited for new knowing or many like them. The consciousness to transcend that habit and hold oneself in the ambiguity with more and more questions, more and more information, more and more confusion leads to an instant when our collective mind comes to know that we have made a discovery together that none of us could have made alone.

Building a Collective Commitment

Continual cocreation in community works, and it works best when the whole system has learned how to be comfortable with chaos. Continual cocreation in community or any other form of self-organization that produces consistent, effective, and beneficial results for the organization cannot occur if just one person is trying to make it work. It matters not where in the organization that one person is.

Building an organization with the capacity for the dynamic re-creating of itself around whatever conditions are delivered to it is a system project. The system may be quite small, but it is something that a system does as its collective work. A committee of three or four can engage cocreation in community around a single project. A department can engage in cocreation in community around a special project or even achieve it in its regular, daily operations as the general rule. Larger work units have the potential for integrating cocreation in more of their work than smaller ones, simply because generally larger units operate more autonomously more of the time.

To *maximize* the effectiveness of any cocreative system, a serious review of policies and practices and adoption of new systems that support the new way of working are in order. It isn't mandatory, but it definitely improves the chances of sustaining long-term change. Often this is possible only when the whole organization makes the commitment to change. At a minimum, this will mean new expectations about how people are selected, reviewed, and rewarded that support cocreation and both collective and individual risk taking. A dialogue that explores the unwritten rules of the organization always provides enlightening materials to guide the transformation process.

Long-term, large-scale change transpires more easily and more completely when managers and employees are committed to transforming their way of working together. A large-scale commitment allows them to invest serious time and attention to figuring out what cocreation in a community will mean for their work group specifically and what new skills, abilities, norms, and support systems will be required to facilitate the change.

Even one person can make a difference. A single individual can take others to their not-knowing simply by asking curious, open-ended questions. Others need not even know what is occurring. Often, a single person can engage others in an effective dialogue that produces new meaning and understanding without the other(s) knowing what is occurring. The comment of one workshop participant after a day of learning dialogue skills is typical of ones I often hear, "I have lived next to my neighbor for 12 years, and last night we had the first meaningful conversation we've had in that time."

When we improve the quality of our interactions, we begin to diminish the walls of our fears and the fears of others. Dialogue inevitably takes people to a level from which they see commonalities rather than differences. It takes people to a place where they begin to feel connection and common meaning and purpose. When we feel deep connection and common meaning and purpose, our defensiveness diminishes and our unspoken fears begin to melt.

In a world of constant change, it is critical that we learn how to embrace the chaos delivered to us and to create chaos if it isn't there. Knowing is the most dangerous place in which to be. Fearing and resisting chaos and not-knowing will take us only deeper into it. We can go to not-knowing individually, and we can individually take others there. Collectively, we can do it more effectively. Our individual and collective questions usually force others from their trances and take them to their not-knowing for at least a moment. Knowing *is* the most dangerous place in which to be. We owe it to ourselves and all of our relationships, including the one with our work, to regularly embrace the chaos of not-knowing.

Transforming the Fear

- By definition, in chaos, systems become completely unpredictable. Yet, despite the inevitable unpredictability, most managers respond to chaos by trying to take control. Although chaos, by nature, is uncontrollable, order is implicit in chaos, and chaos is implicit in order. Our demands for predictability have become our insurance of mediocrity.

- In a world of continuous change, 21st century workplaces will best accomplish tasks by working in a state of continual cocreation in community. Cocreation involves the whole system in open, respectful relationships, engaging in a free flow of information around a common sense of purpose, until it understands its task well enough to organize itself most effectively around the project at hand.
- Cocreation requires that the group embrace the chaos and hold itself in not-knowing long enough to reach the point where chaos and order overlap. Here, the group will collectively learn the best way to accomplish its current work. This is best accomplished with a "beginner's mind" that asks open, curious, and naive questions, which build the group's collective intelligence.
- Groups that have a clear sense of self-identity, an understanding of the human and process relationships in the system, and a free flow of information to tell them what is needed develop an incredible capacity to re-create themselves without external direction.
- Even though we expect positive outcomes when we enter into cocreation, being in not-knowing will require us to face fear. Any time we encounter information that will cause us to give up a belief about how the world is, we experience fear until it becomes clear how we will survive in this new world. The uneasiness of the chaos may tempt us to move back to what we believed we knew. That is why emotional competence is so critical.

6

Transforming Our Relationship to Fear

"Within the dimension where life is in chaos, where endless possibilities scramble over one another to become manifest, the Magician reaches within and finds the moment of quiet stillness—the stillpoint. The point before becoming this or that. The Magician harnesses the energy by opening her heart and through love, creates the life's dream of her own choosing."

                                            . . . UNKNOWN

Ralph slams his hand on the bar as he begins to tell his story to the guys at the neighborhood pub. "I knew it would happen. I just knew it would happen. The minute they started talking about that team stuff, I knew the company was looking for a way to cut expenses. They said they wanted to improve quality, but when they let the operators start making decisions, I knew they were going to get rid of a lot of us long-time managers because we were costing 'em too much money."

He continued, "I don't know what this world is coming to. A guy gives a company 28 years of his life, and this is what happens. It's happening everywhere. Whatever happened to loyalty? I gave this company the best years of my life. I worked hard and put in long hours while my kids were growing up, and this is what I get—two weeks vacation pay and a pink slip!"

Ralph thinks he is a victim: he thinks that he was downsized out of a job because he was costing the company too much money. Although the company was hoping to cut costs and improve efficiency, Ralph's bosses never intended that he was a line-item to be cut. In fact, because he hated to fire a long-term, loyal employee, Ralph's immediate boss, Ted, agonized for several weeks before finally making the decision. But, no matter how Ted looked at it, Ralph was just unwilling to grow, change, and try new ways of working.

Ralph's failure to acknowledge his fear of becoming expendable at the outset of organizational change caused that fear to drive his behavior and produce actions and inaction that ultimately led to his job loss. Ralph was unable to recognize, acknowledge, and learn from his fear. This denial behavior resulted from trance states created in the past to help him get through fearful situations he was unable to experience consciously.

Ralph's autopilot response was to do what had always worked for him: take control of the situation and show his superiors that he was capable of taking charge. He threw himself into problems, did a really good job of analyzing the situation, developed a strategy for responding, and then gave orders. Although he did not consciously articulate it, his strategy was contrived to make him the hero by making him look good to his superiors. The assumption was that they would see how important he was, and *his* job would be safe, even as others may be losing theirs.

The problem is that not only Ralph's company but much of the world is discovering that everybody has important information to provide in identifying and solving problems. To improve quality and cut costs, the day of the solo hero had to give way to a team of heroes, each with his or her own important piece.

His autopilot strategy of making himself look good demonstrated his inability to be part of a team that was building its collective intelligence. He was caught in a trance that told him that, to be secure, he alone should have the answers.

In his inability or unwillingness to look at his fears, Ralph missed some very important learning. He failed to recognize that there *was* an important role for him in the new organizational system, but it was a different role. Instead of being the "answer man," effective team leaders ask questions and coach team members; they facilitate communication with other departments, suppliers, and customers; and they become the team's servant leaders. They "plow the soil" for cocreation in community to occur. But, in his fear-induced trance, Ralph couldn't see any of this—all he could do is what he'd always done in an era that no longer existed.

Naming Fear Breaks the Trance

When we choose to consciously name our fears and use them as tools for learning, we break ourselves out of our trance states. We transform our relationship to fear. Rather than allowing unnamed forces to drive us into destructive strategies born of situations in a different time and place, naming our fears keeps us in present time. In present time we can use our creativity and our intellect to learn more about the situations and identify important considerations and possibilities that would have been overlooked without our "fear reminder." When they are named, our fears allow us to make conscious decisions with all the information in the open.

If Ralph had been consciously acknowledging his fears and using them as gifts of learning, he probably would have done many things differently. To start with, he would have asked many more questions about the new role. He may have asked for additional training or coaching. He might even have started assessing his experiences to see where he had experience for this new role, like when he coached his daughter's Little League team and helped sponsor his son's Junior Achievement club in high school.

He may even have sought the help of the company's employee assistance counselor to help him with the psychological adjustment to his new role. But all of these require a not-knowing mind-set. Ralph's trance told him his security was in what he knew so he didn't go to not-knowing.

Fear always is with us. The transformation process doesn't include pretending that we have no fear. Rather, we must embrace fear as a tool for learning and growth. When we name our fear, it will almost always take us to not-knowing for at least a short while and allow us to gather information that will facilitate our internal self-organizational processes. These, in turn, will help us come to know what the change means for us and what different behaviors we must adopt to thrive.

If Ralph had honestly acknowledged his fears, he would have admitted that he was afraid he would get the ax. He would have started asking himself questions to generate more information about the situation; in this case, what the downsizing is about. Such information would be unlikely to surface without this process, most particularly if the individual involved reacted by going into a defensive posture. Ralph's defensive trance reaction was to believe that people with long tenure and high salaries were being fired to save money, so he'd better protect himself by proving how valuable he was.

The inquisitive response, however, is quite different. We first generate more information by asking ourselves questions that challenge our most basic assumptions. Questions that probe our world of certainty include these:

- What if the opposite were true?
- What if those weren't the people getting the ax?
- What if many of the people getting the ax had been there a long time, but that wasn't why they were being fired?
- What if they were getting the ax because they had been unable to change?
- What if they were locked into hierarchy and wouldn't let those who worked for them work as teams in which everyone was a leader?

- What if they were getting the ax because they wouldn't try anything new without turning to their superiors for "permission"?

In an inquisitive response mode, we continue by asking questions of the team. "What can we do to improve our quality? What can we do to reduce waste? What can we do to cut costs?" When we are able to hold ourselves in not-knowing—knowing that we lack the answers—we open ourselves and our work units to collective learning about the situation. Soon, the inquisitive servant-leader may discover that the department has reduced costs, improved quality, has higher morale and lower absenteeism, has reduced on-the-job injuries, and has come up with some inventive new ways of generating products. The team leader has not done this by conceiving what needed to be done but by getting out of the way of what needed to be done by staying in not-knowing.

Waking from Our Trances

When Ralph denied or failed to acknowledge his fear, he robbed himself of the resources it could have offered him. He also abdicated the responsibility for his personal growth to a fear-driven autopilot trance. Most often, our trances offer limited options, usually drawing on self-reliant behavior that helped us survive a crisis or crises in the past without letting others know we were afraid. Often, we do what Ralph did. He let his fear-induced trance actually lead him to act in a way that created what he feared—his old "reliable" take-charge response demonstrated an inability to change that cost him his job.

Had he used the wide-awake inquisitive response, he would have gained a whole new understanding of his fear and what it would take to stay in his position. By going toward his fear, he would have tried a "higher-risk" strategy, which would have involved finding out what those who reported to him needed from him to work together better as a team. Although this approach would not necessarily ensure that Ralph would have kept his job in all circumstances, it certainly would have improved his chances. Should he have lost his job anyway, his new "management style" with a proven track record of being able to lead a successful team would make him more valuable to other employers. Furthermore, throughout the process, Ralph would have felt like he was in the driver's seat in his life and not reacting as a helpless victim.

Consciously addressing and dealing with our fears most often requires us to acknowledge our fears to others and involve them and other resources in formulating an intentional plan for using the information the fears have given us to move forward in spite of them. The possibilities that Ralph might have explored in developing a strategy to allow him to move toward his fears include asking *others* questions, getting more information about the new role *from others*, requesting training *from others*, and seeking counseling *from others*. What we are doing is cocreating our response to our fear in community with others, consciously and intentionally, giving the company and the individuals involved the full benefit of wide-awake participation.

Perhaps more important, we can initiate this by ourselves. It relieves us of depending on the company to take care of us, thereby helping us grow into new ways of working. In a world of continuous change, the ability to have an inquiring mind, discover new ways of working, and learn how to grow into them is extremely valuable to us personally and to other potential employers.

Resisting What Wants to Happen

Defensive reactions are not unique to individuals. Often, large groups of people within organizations and sometimes whole organizations themselves defensively resist the inevitable forces of change because they are unwilling to consciously address their fears and use them for learning.

Such large-scale defensiveness often occurs because we are looking at a symptom and looking for someone or something to blame instead of consciously discovering the real problem that inevitably is the source of the fear about which no on wants to talk. Two different manifestations of this will describe how defensiveness really keeps us from identifying and learning from the real problem.

XYZ Company is in an industry that has had the luxury of generous profits over the years. These profits allowed it to provide a reasonably indulgent work environment. The era of luxury in the industry is rapidly passing, if it is not already gone. In an effort to cut costs and diversify product offerings, XYZ recently merged with ABC Company. In conjunction with the merger, "downsizing" has eliminated duplicated services and other cost cutting has occurred.

I have had more than one occasion to talk with employees for the merged company, and usually, the conversation turns to blaming corporate officers for being greedy. The employees express a lot of resistance. They want to re-create a work environment "like it used to be." They blame the officers. They blame the merger. "If only, we hadn't merged . . ." they say and then drift back into the illusion that the merger is the problem.

The merger is the symptom. The problem is adjusting to a changing competitive environment to which the company was responding with the merger and downsizing. As long as people focus on the merger and blame others, they will continue to resist changing conditions and attempt to re-create the old work environment in the new, merged company.

An inquisitive response mode might have produced very different attitudes and responses. They might have asked, "Is the merger the change, or is the merger a sign of the change? In this new, more competitive environment, how can we further improve our market position? What did we have in the old work environment that was particularly important to us? How can we sustain that quality while reducing costs?" This kind of active inquiry could have empowered them to realize that they still had a lot of influence over their work environment, as long as they were completely conscious and intentional about creating what they wanted. Instead, hundreds of victims whine and blame the company's officers.

This is not to say that the employees bear all the responsibility for what has occurred in the aftermath of the merger. Certainly, the corporate officers are responsible for how they dealt with their own fears. Afraid of engaging the company in a cocreative process, all changes related to the merger have been autocratic and centralized, with people in one part of the globe unilaterally deciding how things should be throughout the world. Intent on controlling the process, they have created what they feared: they totally lost control of the human element as morale lags and creativity, which is essential in their competitive market, suffers.

Had the corporate officers engaged in an inquisitive process, they might have asked, "What is our most important product? If creativity is our most important product, what must we do to ensure that people remain creative? What conditions foster creativity? What must we do to cut costs *and* foster creativity?"

In almost every corporate readjustment of whatever type, the company carries a significant degree of responsibility in *not* engaging in any cocreative or participative inquiry process. But, for those affected by the changes, blaming the organization for not doing its part will do nothing for us as individuals affected by them. We gain our power by engaging our own inquisitive, cocreative process that makes us more valuable individuals, either in our current organization that is changing or in a different one, to which we may choose to go for employment.

A Whole Industry Needs to Be Inquisitive

One reason it is so critical for us individually to learn how to deal with our fear and engage it in cocreative inquiry, rather than depend on a company to do so, is because often the company can't.

A company that is denying its own fear is incapable of taking supportive actions such as those that would result from a cocreative process.

One of the most graphic examples of a whole industry's inability to support the devastation that occurred in the lives of its employees and their families is in the American automobile industry. Its historical denial of its fear has been characterized by looking for something outside itself for its lack of international competitiveness.

When imports began to flood the United States in the late 1960s and 1970s, the industry took several years to get the message that Americans wanted better-quality, fuel-efficient economy in vehicles. They were looking at a symptom, Japanese manufacturers, rather than the problem, poor quality and economy, that created a market for other manufacturers. A quarter of a century later, the tables turned and American automakers wanting to sell cars in Japan blamed trade barriers for their inability to sell automobiles there. Granted, there have been trade barriers, but Japanese people will tell you that, except for status symbol cars, they don't want to buy American cars because they don't perceive them to be well made.

Instead of immediately looking for someone to blame, if the industry had started with identifying the problem—automakers weren't making cars people wanted to buy if they had alternatives—it could have learned a lot that would have allowed it to respond more consciously, more quickly, and with more focus. If automakers had gone to not-knowing, instead of thinking of themselves as victims looking for something to blame, they would have discovered a lot of important information that otherwise took them a number of years to learn. "What makes people *want* to buy Japanese cars? What do Japanese cars offer that we don't? What would it take for us to offer the same thing? What would it take for us to offer more? Does what is going on have anything to do with Japanese cars or is it really about our cars?" Instead of asking these sorts of questions, they waited for the government to force fuel standards and for Japanese manufacturers to build high-quality cars in the United States. If these American manufacturers had faced their fears, they would have discovered what their responsibility was and what they must do to accept that responsibility. With such information in hand, they could have taken the offensive and saved 25 years lost in trance-state reactivity, blaming, and hand-wringing.

It is important for us as human beings to be more emotionally competent and experience more wholeness at work, but it is an effectiveness issue as well. Our organizations work better when people are awake and using all the information, including that provided by their emotions, to make decisions and respond to our ever-changing world.

Discovering New Life

When people learn to name and honor fear for the gift it gives, magic happens. We learn important things about a situation that previously we may have missed or see new response possibilities. Incredible positive energy and emotion are released that become fire for what we are doing. We get the whole person. Instead of trying to get more out of people, we allow more to bubble forth from within them as they wake up to their own potential and possibilities.

Had Ralph been willing to consciously address his fears, he may have experienced one of the most exciting and energizing periods of his life. He may have discovered capabilities, skills, talents, and gifts in himself of which he had been unaware. He could have experienced joy and delight in seeing those who had been his subordinates learn new skills and discover new talents. Increased satisfaction may have emerged as the team identified pieces of a problem puzzle that he might have overlooked.

Similarly, the merged ABC/XYZ Company could have initiated a process whereby it intentionally maintained the work-environment qualities people truly valued, while cutting costs, by engaging employees in a cocreation process that could have been exhilarating. Likewise, a fully awake and eagerly responsive automobile industry could have given itself new life decades ago.

Quite often, such rewarding outcomes help us discover new energy for life after work. We develop the confidence and courage to do something that we've always wanted to do, be it learn a foreign language, a musical instrument, an athletic pursuit, or ballroom dancing.

Creating a Ripple

The ripple effect of learning how to recognize and use fear and developing emotional competence in the workplace reaches our personal lives as well. Even though this sometimes creates a period of awkwardness at home as the family begins to acknowledge its own denial systems, people repeatedly report stories of improved relationships at home. One woman said, "I had the best conversation with my 16-year-old son that I've ever had." A CEO reported that his wife said to him, "There's something about you that is different. I don't know what it is, but you're just more . . . open." Another man related having his first meaningful conversation with a neighbor of 12 years.

When we learn to honor and respect our own emotions, we almost simultaneously begin to develop the ability to listen to, accept, honor, and respect the feelings of others. We may need to build some skills and practice, but we immediately will begin to wake up in our relationships.

Transforming Fear by Transforming Our Relationship to It

To change our relationship to fear, we must adopt a different perspective. We have been talking about acknowledgment and acceptance, but the balance lies in shifting two other perspectives. First, we must switch from a protective perspective to a commitment to learning. As long as we are concerned about how we are going to recover, recoup, survive, respond, or make some kind of reactive response to what happens, we will view all that we do from a place of protection. Any time we are in a protective mind-set, we automatically will go to a primitive fight-or-flight reaction.

Both personally or organizationally, we must change the nature of our commitment to a specific outcome to one of learning from whatever outcome occurs and how to find joy in it. We must stop automatically reacting, out of the fight-or-flight trance, and instead find ourselves consciously choosing how we will be in relationship to whatever is occurring, as it is happening. We must choose a relationship of learning in all we do.

When we choose a relationship of learning from all outcomes, simultaneously, we realize no decisions are wrong. The only way a decision can be "wrong" is in its execution, not in its content. The commitment is to learning the lesson we are to learn, not to a specific outcome. We transform our relationship to what happens, thereby transforming our need for fear. If we believe it possible for something bad to happen, then we have cause to fear. If we know that the purpose of whatever occurs is for us to learn, then we have nothing to fear because whatever occurs is exactly what was supposed to occur for us to learn the lessons we learned.

Not-knowing is where this kind of "living in lesson" occurs. Because we do not and cannot know what particular lesson we are to learn at any time, we must hold ourselves in not-knowing about both a decision and what we will learn from its outcomes. We do know that, for an organization to be awake, part of the learning involves doing the work of the enterprise more consciously, focusing on knowing what lesson we are to learn. We must consciously ask ourselves, "Are we learning?" and "Did we learn?" We must be joyful and enthusiastic about the learning process, knowing that there are no bad decisions or outcomes, only lessons. Thus, the business of the enterprise changes from just making widgets or taking care of sick people or selling hamburgers. The new work of our organizations is to be conscious about our relationship to what occurs, to be more awake in our relationships to both our work and our coworkers, and to be in a state of continuous and conscious learning. From this perspective, there are no losing situations or bad decisions. The only failure is the failure to learn and to learn with total, complete, and conscious joy in whatever occurs.

Putting the "If Only . . ." Trance to Rest

The second change in perspective that must occur is to recognize that we can't change others or conditions; we can change only ourselves and how we are in relationship with those others and conditions. This shift enables us to awaken from our "if only . . ." trance, in which we become the victims of the actions of others and circumstances beyond our control, and to regain our power to transform any situation. Regaining power is not controlling, because control continues to be an illusion. It is more akin to "making lemonade" when we are dealt lemons. When we are open to changing our relationship to what occurs, oftentimes we discover that the lemons actually led to a better end than the one for which we originally hoped. When we are open to changing our relationship to what occurs, even if lemons don't produce a better outcome, we always garner important learning from what does occur.

A number of years ago, when my husband and I were in the earlier stages of changing our relationship to events that were occurring, we took what had the potential to have been the "vacation from hell." We are good trip organizers and had invested a significant amount of time and attention to planning an itinerary, locating places to stay, and making reservations. On this trip, without fail, there was a problem with every piece of the plan. Had we been intent on making the vacation be what we had planned, I am totally convinced that we would have come home frustrated, stressed, and exhausted by our resistance.

Instead, we allowed ourselves to laugh and experience joy in each problem as it occurred while also allowing ourselves to be open to alternatives. In every case, Plan B ended up exceeding our original plan's expectations. At the end of our vacation, we were relaxed and fascinated with our adventure. At some point, we actually started looking forward to things not going according to plan because the alternatives had been so delightful. It was an important lesson that I am sure neither one of us will ever forget.

I have seen similar pleasure in organizations, as clients described to me something that initially seemed to go wrong but eventually was seen as a strong positive. Midway through some major cultural change work in one company, a key executive resigned. This individual was loved and almost revered, and people were openly fearful about what would happen to the company if she quit. A year later, people were trying to figure out what she did. Two years later, people realized that most of what she had done was dysfunctional and her leaving was the best thing that ever happened to the company.

Discovering the Magician in Each of Us

In the psychological alchemy process, we begin life as an Innocent who believes he or she cannot be hurt because hurt has never been experienced. The culminating stage is that of the Magician, who shares much in common with the Innocent. However, Innocents believe they cannot be hurt because they have never been hurt, while Magicians know they cannot be hurt because being hurt has become a state of mind. From the Magician's perspective, everything can be transformed into a gift. What happens has not changed, but our experience of it changes. So, events about which we have been fearful may still occur, but when our experience of them changes, we have transformed our relationship to fear.

Let's take a person who has been fired from a job and feels like a victim, blaming the company, foreign competition, or the state of modern management practices. He is engaging in neurotic suffering about his firing. He is stuck in his ego and what he believes he knows, and he is miserable there. He can see no other way to experience the event except one in which he is a victim. He has gone through life being fearful. This incident is seen as proof positive that the universe is not a friendly place, so he had better go through the rest of life in a guarded manner, making sure that no one hurts him.

A person in the Magician stage of development who is fired may see it as an opportunity to make a transition into doing different work that he or she has longed to do. This may be to start a business or just to try something different. The individual is likely to still suffer a blow to the ego but is able to transform a brief period of neurotic suffering into one of transcendent suffering. This individual sees the incident as a gift from God, a Guardian Angel, the Universe, or whatever exists beyond oneself. The firing becomes an opportunity. The Magician has choice in determining the meaning of the event.

Becoming My Own Magician

After 20 years of being employed by others, I chose to start my own business. I was accustomed to having a regular paycheck and benefits, so I had a great deal of uneasiness about my ability to support myself in the beginning. When I was being unconsciously afraid that I wouldn't survive if I were self-employed, I conformed my work to every potential client's comfort level and attempted to "close the sale." It didn't work. This was deep and personal work, and those who were not ready just weren't ready. When I repackaged the work into a tastier medicine, I was less effective because we weren't doing the *real* work.

Finally, I gave it up. I acknowledged several fears, but like so many of my clients, survival and approval of others were at the core. About that time, I had lunch with a friend of mine who had recently been downsized out of a middle management job. She admitted to having some relief at the termination because she felt that she had been forced to compromise her integrity in the position. "I can always drive a truck," she said. Not to be disparaging toward truck drivers, but my friend used that to symbolize that there were a lot of ways to earn a living that wouldn't compromise her integrity. She didn't want to be in that position again.

Although she had come to me as part of a networking project to find a new job, she gave me an incredible gift of freedom. I realized that taking work I didn't feel good about was my way of compromising my own integrity, and I didn't like it. I did it because I was afraid I couldn't survive if I didn't. Suddenly, I realized that there were hundreds of jobs I could do if I just wanted to survive, but I didn't want to just survive. I wanted to thrive, and I wasn't going to do that taking work that I didn't feel called to do.

After that, whenever work didn't come my way, I decided that the potential client would find someone who was more suited to that firm's readiness and that space was being made for a more rewarding project. A more rewarding project almost always came. When it didn't, I allowed myself to use the time for a writing project, like this one, that I had wanted to do for a long time. At one time, a gap in my work certainly would have produced great fear in me. Now it produces joy in me. The circumstances are the same; I choose to experience them differently.

I would be lying if I were to say that I have no fear as I sit here with a calendar that has far fewer bookings than usual. I do have fear; I just haven't allowed myself to become the fear. In fact, I intentionally moved toward this fear. A couple of years ago I was living in a part of the country in which the climate just didn't suit me. I had a young but booming local consulting practice, and for the first time since I had started the business, the potential to enjoy the fruits of my labor was on the horizon.

At the same time, I realized that I would never be at my peak in a climate that was cool, damp, and either foggy or rainy for most of the year. So, even though I knew that moving would mean leaving behind most of my clientele and starting over, I chose to do so. I know many people who would like to do the same, but they have lots of reasons why they "can't": the reasons all spell that they are frozen from moving by their fear. If they moved and didn't have work for a few weeks, they would probably panic. I discovered an opportunity to write a book I was passionate about doing.

Instead of "knowing" that I was to be consulting and being frightened that I'd starve because I wasn't, I held myself in "not-knowing" until it became clear to me that this was space provided in which to write a book.

Tapping the Power of Our Intentions

In addition to opening ourselves to new possibilities offered by unexpected outcomes, when we are able to name our fear, we avail ourselves of the power of our intentions. We can design what we want from our actions on all levels. Not being locked to a specific outcome, we are able to engage in meaningful dialogue about acting within our values and meeting our personal and organizational needs while we are "in lesson." When it isn't hidden behind a veil of secrecy, our emotional data almost always will point to important considerations for our process. We are then able to give voice to our intentions, allowing them to lead us consciously and openly through our learning process, while addressing concerns about respecting people, valuing differences, communicating openly, and other apprehensions our members may have.

If we are afraid that a major expansion of our business will cause our quality to suffer and perhaps jeopardize our values, naming those fears allows us to be able to give specific attention to them. Furthermore, we are able to express our intention to undertake the expansion in a way that ensures high quality and faithfulness to our values. Explicit attention then can be given to devising a plan that safeguards these important aspects of the organization.

Incredible transformational power lies in clearly cocreating what we intend and the consciousness-raising process that accompanies this activity. It is power that energizes and builds commitment. When I do this kind of activity with a group, I usually ask them to imagine that their organization was a legendary one, to which both the press and professional community would turn to discover how to build better workplaces. Then, I have them define with hundreds of details what it would look like and be like to work in that kind of enterprise. What starts as stretching their envelopes often evolves into exploding their envelopes as they discover little separates what they are from where they want to be. Although little that is tangible may separate them from what they want to be, the "little" is significant, for it is formed largely of the attitudes, assumptions, beliefs, relationships, and habits that keep them locked into the current system. The courage to consciously and intentionally change those impediments lies principally in being able to name and transform the fears that gave rise to them in the first place.

The key questions usually will come some time later, when I ask, "What would you personally have to do differently to be in this legendary organization?" And, "What would it take for you to be willing to commit to doing that?" This is when they face their individual fears, and most make a commitment to working differently. The critical component of this exercise is that people must quit their "if only . . ." and "blaming" trances and recognize that each has the personal power to create the kind of workplace in which they want to spend their time.

Along the way, these individuals will grapple with how their new relationships will look: what the relationship to themselves will be, what the relationship to their work will be, what the relationship to their coworkers, peers, "bosses" and subordinates will be, and finally what their relationship to fear in their lives and the world will be. As they consciously express their intention to change their relationship to fear in each of those cases, they give power to their intention to be different in the world and at work. In the process, they organize themselves and come to that new level of knowing from which change occurs as discovery is made. Implementation of the new behaviors begins before they leave the room.

Transforming the Fear

- Rather than allowing unnamed forces to drive us into destructive strategies born of situations in a different time and place, naming our fears keeps us in present time, gives us access to important learning, and allows us to use our creativity and intellect to learn more about the situation.
- The process of transforming fear isn't pretending that we have no fear but embracing fear as a tool for learning and growth.
- Asking questions about our fears helps us challenge our most basic assumptions about how things are. In a world of continuous change, having an inquiring mind, discovering new ways of working, and learning how to grow into them is extremely valuable to us personally and collectively.
- The ripple effect of learning how to appreciate fear and developing emotional competence in the workplace reaches our personal lives as well. Even though this may create a period of awkwardness as the family begins to acknowledge its own denial systems, over the long term it transforms personal relationships, too.
- As we become emotionally competent, two life perspectives must change:

  We must switch from a protective perspective to one of commitment to learning.

  We must recognize that we can't change others or conditions; we can change only ourselves and how we are in relationship with those others and conditions.

- When we are willing to talk about what we fear and what outcomes we want, we avail ourselves of the power of our intentions. We can design what we want from our actions on all levels, while not being locked into a specific result.

7

Performing the Magic

"What this power is I cannot say; all I know is that it
exists and it becomes available only when a man is in that
state of mind in which he knows exactly what he wants
and is fully determined not to quit until he finds it."

... ALEXANDER GRAHAM BELL

Magic appears to be a mysterious art performed by someone
with supernatural abilities. When we watch a magician at work,
he or she appears mystically to be making things happen that are
not possible. Yet, if we are able to talk honestly with people who
perform magic tricks, they will tell you what they are doing is
not really mysterious at all. They learn a set of steps required to
perform a trick. They learn special "tips" that make it appear
mysterious. They try it a few times, usually with a more experienced practitioner, to gain confidence that they can perform the
trick. Then, they practice, practice, practice refining their skill
and developing confidence. Eventually, they master the trick.

When someone masters an activity that only a limited number of people do well, what he or she does has a magical quality.

For 25 years, gourmet cooking has been my hobby, and I delight in sharing it with people who appreciate food. I am no practitioner of kitchen voodoo that allows me to perform feats that surpass normal human ability, but the reactions I often get would seem as if others have credited me with magical abilities. I simply read cookbooks, follow instructions, dump out a lot of failures, and practice making and modifying the recipes I like. I know that, when I put myself into the frame of mind to make something, I can do it, even if it takes a few false starts before I get there. I expect failures. I expect to learn from mistakes and get better over time. My friends see magic. There is no magic, just following steps in a process and practice.

A year ago when I started learning ballroom dancing, I watched more experienced dancers, and I just knew that they had some mysterious natural gift that allowed them to perform feats of magic on the dance floor. I knew that I would never be that good, but that wasn't my goal. I just wanted to have fun dancing socially. In the beginning, it was terribly hard. I worked for hours and hours just trying to master one turn. I was certain that I would never get it. Never. But I was determined. This was something I had wanted to do for most of my life. I knew what I wanted, and I wasn't going to give up. I practiced and I practiced. My ego argued for me to give up. I was doing embarrassing things, like stepping on other people's feet.

The frustration was intense at times, when I knew what I wanted to do and simply could not make my body do it. Then, I did it once. Then, I did it again. As if by magic, I was doing it again and again. Then, I couldn't figure out how I hadn't been able to do it. One step at a time, one turn at a time, I added to my repertoire. Suddenly, I discovered if I was relaxed and open to learning, I could dance with partners who led steps I didn't know, and I was able to do them without practice! I remember well one evening when I realized suddenly that I was a dancer. It felt natural and easy—and magical. Then, I started noticing some of the people I had credited with magical abilities a few months earlier. I realized that I was nearly as good as they were. There was no magic. It was simply determination, willingness to make lots of mistakes, and practice, practice, practice.

Some people treat the ability to face their fears and do things they have never done before in the same way my friends do my cooking or I did more experienced dancers. They think there is a secret ability or mysterious gift. They seem to think that people who do things that require courage have no fear or have a magical ability that allows them not to feel their fears. I don't know of anyone who is sane who doesn't experience fear. Some of us simply have the determination to move toward our fears, and we practice learning what we need to do that. There is no magic. There is simply determination, willingness to make lots of mistakes, and practice, practice, practice.

So it is with the alchemy of fear. Transforming our relationship with fear isn't magic. It need not be mysterious. What we need to do is understand what is required to change any set of behaviors and beliefs about what is possible, consciously commit to becoming something different from what we have been, and discover what we know about what that will require of us. After that, we need only determination, willingness to make lots of mistakes, and practice, practice, practice.

Becoming

We all have an image of who we think we are. Most of it was created by our egos, often in conjunction with the socialization process. I recently talked with a man who told me he was into his fifties before he figured out that he wasn't at all the person he thought he was. A few months after he took up meditation, he began to realize that almost everything he did in his life was because someone else had told him or showed him that was the way he should be. The food he ate and the clothes he wore were those selected by people around him. The way he thought about things was determined largely by the people with whom he had grown up and later went to college and graduate school. Some of the things he was afraid of doing were things that others around him had done and either he or they had judged the outcomes as unsatisfactory, so he had chosen not to engage in those activities.

When he began being aware that he had other options, he was able to choose to become something else. Now in his seventies, Bob has been engaging in a 20-year process, which is far from complete, of becoming who he is. He didn't sit down one day and say, "This is who I am," and instantly change. He began a moment-by-moment process of becoming aware of what he was doing at any time, then consciously choosing what felt right for him because he wanted it, not because that was the way he had always done it. He is becoming who he is.

Bob still dresses pretty much the same way he always did. The clothes are comfortable. He finds he eats less meat now because he is aware that he feels better when he doesn't. In fact, he finds he feels better eating more simply than how he was accustomed to eating.

He talks about how he is feeling a lot more than he did before. When he is being fully who he is, it makes space for others to become who they are, and he finds himself experiencing deeper connections with people. He says it has not been easy, because he now realizes how much of his life had been habit. But as he consciously practices listening to his inner guidance, he is fully becoming Bob.

Bob's process is not unlike what I have watched in both individuals and groups wrestling with the magical process of transforming their relationship with fear. The individual or individuals within a group become aware of how much of what they do occurs in trance states driven by fear. They begin noticing fear-driven behaviors in themselves and others. They begin to notice that they rarely walk toward what they want but often choose a particular path because it takes them away from outcomes they are afraid of generating. Then they begin choosing to consciously do it differently, each hour, each day, each week. There is no magic—simply determination, willingness to make lots of mistakes, and practice, practice, practice. They are learning moment by moment how to become what they want to be, individually and organizationally.

There is a lot of frustration in the beginning, not unlike what I experienced when I spent so many hours trying to learn one dance turn and felt like I was never going to get it. But, just like I learned with that troublesome dance turn, one day in what often feels like a miraculous moment, we find ourselves being what we wanted to become. By commitedly practicing, day in and day out, we have moved from awareness to working and living more consciously.

At this point, people move a little slower. They are taking time to be more thoughtful. When they find themselves sliding into trance behavior, they may stop midstream and change course. When they don't catch themselves until later, they reflect back on the situation, determining how they might have acted differently. Sometimes they go back to others and initiate a replay of a conversation or a decision. In the consciousness stage, they become aware of how important it is to be fully in the present, because they usually have discovered in the awareness stage that many of their trances were conceived to either address conditions in the past that no longer exist or prepare for dreaded catastrophes that have yet to occur.

In the consciousness stage, people begin to give up the illusion of control. They learn to express their fears and intentionally plan a course of action that will address them. This plan is focused on how they are in relationship to their fear. It does not establish an attachment to a specific outcome. They check regularly when they catch themselves or others slipping into the past or the future. They ask questions like "Are we doing everything we planned to do?" "Have conditions changed in a way that requires us to change our plan?" "Are we meeting the spirit of our values?" "Are we producing top-quality products today?" "Have we done everything we must to produce top-quality products tomorrow?" In the inquisitive mode, they are able to detect when course adjustments need to be made and consciously and intentionally do so, while avoiding knee-jerk actions that result from reaction to unnamed fears. They begin to have faith that, if they are doing what they need to be doing moment by moment, the long term will take care of itself.

The Psychology of Becoming

The ego is designed to protect us. It is the self-centered part of us that believes us to be separate from others and any divine support system. Much like the Orphan archetype that we've discussed, the ego believes the world poses a threat to us, so it needs to take care of us. As a consequence, it has a lot invested in having us be what we have been. Because we have survived in that mode, it believes this is the only safe existence for us. It also believes that if we chose to function differently in the world, we would perish.

Because the ego's function is to keep us alive, it resists learning new ways of being, often vehemently. But, it usually does so in very subtle ways: a slip of the tongue, forgetting to do something that supports what we are becoming, or sliding back into old habits. Oddly enough, sometimes, when we have made significant progress toward becoming what we want to be, we will fall back into old habits that seem to come from nowhere. After several weeks of dancing in the magical mode—long enough that it was beginning to feel normal—suddenly I couldn't seem to even walk, much less dance, without stepping on my own feet. I couldn't seem to do anything right. The part of me that thought it couldn't be a dancer, that was embarrassed when I even tried, just didn't want to give up. I hope that was its last vestige of life, but it was not going to give up without a last gasp at sustaining my supposed respectability.

At this stage, we feel inner conflict about who we are. The ego identifies with what we've always been, how we've always lived, and the way we learned to survive, usually by not taking significant risks. It is confident and knows that we can "make it" being that person. Yet, part of us is the person we are becoming, someone who experiences connection to everyone else, nature, and a deeper wisdom that knows we can do anything. This is our spirit—the source of faith in ourselves and others, hope, joy, and enthusiasm for life. It wants to thrive. It wants to live life by choosing what it wants to be rather than by choosing what it doesn't want to be.

The development of a healthy ego is critical. We actually could not survive without it. However, we have evolved to the point that, for many of us, the ego isn't a healthy part of our lives. Its Orphan-like fearfulness drives our lives. Because our human development attends first to basic survival issues, the ego has been dominant for most of our lives. We have fallen into a trance that has led us to believe that this is all there is. Consequently, for most of us, the spirit or our Magician archetype is far less experienced in calling the shots in our lives and therefore far less confident.

Any time we attempt anything new that is not fear driven, the inner conflict between these two forces will ensue for anywhere from hours to months, depending on how fearful what we want to become is to us. Every time we choose to become something different than what we have been, the historically dominant part will resist giving up what it perceives to be its only means of survival. Regardless of how small or how large the change, this part is afraid of perishing. It is in a life-or-death battle, for it knows that, when we discover we can survive living in a more expansive way, we will never again choose the limitations that have enslaved us. Figure 7-1 illustrates the internal conflict between what we have been and what we are becoming.

At the point where the two are roughly the same strength, the part we have been resists most vociferously. That is when it realizes that its dominance, even its existence in our lives, is threatened. It is also when we are most tempted to slide back into old habits and unconscious living.

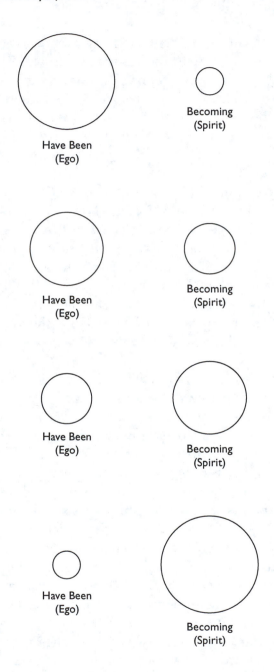

Figure 7-1   *Have Been and Becoming*

The Granddaddy of All Fears

More often than not, we treat this internal resistance to change with frustration, irritation, and even anger. Usually subconsciously, but sometimes consciously, we are afraid that who we want to become will succumb to who we have been. So our fear of not changing is engaged in a life-and-death battle with our fear of changing.

When children are frightened, we will usually acknowledge their fear, comfort them, maybe hold them, and assure them we will help them. Depending on the age of the child, we may talk with them about what is happening and help them to understand that they are going to be all right. Few of us would respond to a frightened child with anger, impatience, or irascibility, and if it is something that the child really needs to learn to do, few of us would respond by surrendering to the fear.

Yet, the part of us that is afraid of changing is much like that child. It needs to be loved, comforted, and reassured that there is a different way of surviving. It needs to know more about how we plan to survive when we become who we want to be. It needs to know what we have to gain from being different. We don't need to give up, we just need to be compassionate and patient.

It is important at this point to remind the reader that fear is a primitive emotion that far predates the development of our rational brains, so often, we will have fears that are not rational by nature. This is why it is absolutely essential that we develop a process whereby we can bring the irrational into the light of rationality. Working with individuals and groups, I have found that one deep, underlying fear is the foundation of all others: the fear of not surviving. The rational brain would tell most of us that the success or failure of a particular new work initiative is not life threatening, but this fear is housed in a more primitive part of the brain and is not rational.

So, members of the management team that is afraid of losing market share may discover that peeling the onion of their fears produces the following revelations:

What are you afraid of?
> I am afraid that we are going to lose market share to ABC Company if we don't beat them to market with this new product.

What would you be afraid of then?
> Our regular customers would go to ABC for other products as well.

What would you be afraid of then?
> We could not remain competitive.

What would you be afraid of then?
> The company wouldn't survive.

What would you be afraid of then?
> A lot of people would lose their jobs.

What would you be afraid of then?
> I would lose my job.

What would you be afraid of then?
> I would lose my house.

What would you be afraid of then?
> I couldn't find another job.

What would you be afraid of then?
> I would be unable to take care of my family.

What would you be afraid of then?
> I would lose my family.

What would you be afraid of then?
> I would be alone.

What would you be afraid of then?
> I would be unable to take care of myself.

What would you be afraid of then?
> I would end up like a street person.

What would you be afraid of then?
> I might freeze to death or starve.

As irrational as it may seem to read, I have done this process with too many people not to believe that the granddaddy of most of our fears is fear of our inability to survive. A large percentage of the people with whom I do this process end up seeing themselves homeless, hungry, and alone, and that fear subconsciously drives much of what they do.

One early reader of this manuscript denied that he went to a core survival fear, instead professing to simply want to "survive in a decent manner." This is his denial of his most core fear. Having done this with many people, most will go to a real life-and-death fear of survival. And, that is important to the process.

Articulating this core fear sheds light on the irrationality. It opens a dialogue about what survival means. Naming this core fear also helps us lovingly guide our frightened part to discover that there are other options for survival, when it had believed and had us believing that we had no other possibilities. If we don't have the job we have now, we will end up starving in the streets. Once we get to this core fear, then we can explore it consciously and even do what I call *make friends with the worst case scenario*. If we really are afraid the company will fail because we don't beat the competition to market on this one product, then what possibilities other than starving in the streets are available to us individually?

This work regularly culminates almost blissfully for those who do it. Often an initial reckoning shows that the person could find a similar job in a similar company—maybe even ABC Company. Then, the magic begins. Frequently, the individual relates a story about something he or she has always wanted to do but just hasn't had time, courage, or circumstance to do. The person discovers that this might hold the opening he or she has needed to realize this dream, maybe a dream that never has been articulated to another person.

This process of making peace with the worst case scenario[1] gives the individual the power to fully participate in the job he or she has now. Having now discovered that they could not only survive but possibly even benefit from experiencing the "worst case," people are liberated from their fear of sharing the ideas they have withheld out of concern for others' negative judgment. They are free to explore creative ways for meeting the challenge at hand. They are liberated from doing a mediocre job and freed to do an outstanding job.

When I planned this book, I mapped the fears that I encounter most commonly in workplaces through a sequence like the previous dialogue. It quickly became apparent to me as I did this that all fear is going to the same place; when we peeled the layers away, they were all based in a fear of not surviving. Our fear of change was fear that we wouldn't be able to survive in the new work environment. Our fear of losing our job was fear of not being able to find another job and not being able to survive. Our fear of loss of control was fear that we wouldn't be able to survive if we lost control. Our fear of going out on a limb and trying something new was a fear of being alone and not being able to survive. They were all rooted in the same fear: the fear of not being able to survive.

The power of bringing core fears lovingly to rationality and discovering options, even attractive ones, gives individuals a freedom to pursue their work in the current company that they may never have experienced. The ideas that they've always held back for fear of judgment are shared, and new avenues for getting the product to market ahead of ABC Company bubble forth. I have repeatedly watched groups who are able to openly cocreate because they have explored their fears accomplish tasks in days that normally would take months or even years.

Not surprisingly, we experience one more paradox. Only in discovering the freedom to survive, and even thrive, outside of our current organization can we be fully in it. That happens because we awaken to part of us that is in love with life. When we discover it, we can bring it to what we are doing now.

Bringing Light to Our Fears

The part of us that is afraid of becoming something new feels threatened because we may be asked to do things that we have never done before. We may not only embarrass ourselves, like I often did when I was learning to dance, but we may actually fail. The frightened part of us has the illusion that, if we never try, we never fail. Actually, quite the opposite is true: if we never try, we always fail. We won't grow without trying and risking failure. We must open ourselves to being vulnerable to our own judgment and that of others. The frightened part doesn't know we can survive that vulnerability.

Part of what we would do with a frightened child is to help the child come to know that he or she has the resources to endure in the face of the perceived threat. So, when we are compassionately supporting our frightened part, it should be no surprise to us that discovering the resources that we have, about which we may not have been conscious, is essential to moving forward.

When someone says to me or a group that I am working with, "I don't know," I often reply, "If you did know, what would you know?" With little hesitation, the person begins to tell me a great deal about the very thing about which they had just told me they knew nothing. Simply asking questions about one's fears not only brings them to consciousness and rationality, but it gives us access to our not-knowing, where we discover what we really *do* know but didn't know we knew. This frequently opens the door to creative responses for troubling workplace challenges.

You will remember that the self-organizational process is the way in which, either individually or collectively, we change our worldview and simultaneously come to know what change is required of us to most effectively do our task. The self-organization process provides the part that we are becoming with enough information to propel the process forward, facilitating instantaneous change, really "growing" the little part. The process usually happens over weeks, months, or even years, although sometimes a crisis, like a wake-up call, may generate enough new information for it to happen in minutes or hours. This happened in my neighborhood in the aftermath of the hurricane.

When it happens naturally, the self-organizing process may be slow and frustrating, but when we understand what is occurring, we can accelerate the process. Once again, the power to do so lies in the question. When we ask deeply probing questions, they help us come to understand what we need to intentionally create to avoid realizing our fears. At the same time, they force us to go into our not-knowing, where we are open to learning. Then we can come to know what we already know about coping in the "new world" we are creating. We have had this knowledge even though we may not have been aware of that. We may learn that experiences we've had in other parts of our lives will help us know how to cope. We also may discover beliefs that have limited us were really based on false assumptions.

Just as we would lovingly support a frightened child, we can support ourselves and each other in our process of becoming. When we ask questions, we provide that kind of support by helping ourselves discover more about what will be required of us in the state we are moving toward and consequently muster what may be flagging courage to move ahead.

Secret Ingredients That Allow It to Happen

Giving compassion to the part of us frightened of becoming something new and learning to consciously support that part of us for as long as it takes certainly is a different way of responding to the resistance we feel during our inner conflict. The process may be long, trying, and arduous. To discover the magic of the process of awakening from our trances is not unlike my learning to dance. It takes the commitment that comes only from knowing what we want and "being fully determined not to quit until"[2] we find it. It requires practice that can be described only as a discipline, not unlike learning a sport, a foreign language, or a musical instrument. New behaviors need to become a regular and constant part of our consciousness. A lifetime of living habitual trances is not undone in a week, a month, or even a year. With faith, we keep doing what we know we must, and eventually days, weeks, or months later, the magic "suddenly" happens. We are being what

---

Ingredients for Transforming Fear

- *Awareness.* We first become aware of our trances and our surface fears and learn to probe them to become aware of our subtle, core fears. We become aware that our worldview is just one of many possibilities rather than objective reality.

- *Consciousness.* We work at remaining conscious of when we are experiencing fears, so we can mine our fears for important information. We learn to live and work in a conscious state, being fully awakened from our trances.

- *Commitment.* We lend the transformation the commitment of a discipline, knowing that transcending a lifetime of habit-induced trance behavior will take lots of practice to become conscious living.

- *Courage.* We must have the courage to give up being a victim and blaming and simultaneously reclaim accountability and our power—the power of love.

---

we have been becoming. This is what happened when I "suddenly" was able to dance after months and months of practice.

This is uncomfortable work in our quick-fix society, but all deep personal transformation work is uncomfortable. When I personally started this work, a friend who was "ahead of me" told me it took her two years to fully integrate the changes into her life in a way that she felt she was really living consciously. "Two years!" I thought. I didn't think I could do it, but I was committed. One day at a time, one week at a time, I kept at it. Suddenly, I remember thinking "I'm beginning to think I might get this." At that moment, my friend's comment about two years came to my mind, and I chuckled out loud as I realized that it had been almost exactly two years since I started the work.

I have observed, in both my own process and that of clients and friends, that, to sustain progress, regular reminders to ourselves support our commitment and encourage our success. As I progressed in my own process, more often than not I tended to notice the times I slipped into a trance and overlooked what might have been the 20 or 30 times in between when I stopped my trances and acted consciously. When I noticed I had slipped into a trance, I would be quite impatient with myself, feeling that I was never going to "get it." Two personal reminders kept me going and almost became my mantras during this period. When I caught myself slipping, I would say one of these two reminders to myself:

- "I've had 40 years of practice living in trances. I've been at this only ____ months."
- "So, I goofed up once. How many times have I gotten it right since I last slipped?"

These reminders kept my progress in perspective for me and supported my commitment to change my way of being in relationship to fear.

The final quality I believe is absolutely essential to trans-forming our relationship with fear is courage. This may seem obvious, but I think most people greatly underestimate how much courage it really does take. It was much easier for me to have courage to do my business relationships consciously than it was in my primary relationship. My fear of losing that most impor-tant relationship was much more important to me. Five years down the line, I still find myself slipping into fear on that one.

It is very frightening to enter into and sustain not-knowing for days, weeks, and even sometimes months. The closer is the personal relationship or the more intense our attachment to an outcome, the more frightening it becomes. Sometimes we enter this critical phase with a great deal of courage, which seems to wane as time passes, occasionally reaching the point where we feel we simply cannot sustain it one more minute. Then, we do, because our commitment keeps us going.

One time I was really committed to discovering a new way of being in my primary relationship. Both of us had asked questions and agreed to take some time before answering. Five weeks later, I was almost crazy but committed not to slip into my old trance of "Take all the time you need. Are you ready now?"

The wait was rewarded in several ways. It transformed both the relationship and my role in it more satisfactorily than could have happened otherwise. It also helped me learn a discipline that has been important to my work in businesses.

A former partner and I were taking time out from each other to reassess what the relationship should be. We both loved each other deeply, but we had significant and troubling differences. When I went into our sabbatical, I thought I didn't understand why we had such a difficult time. During our time apart, I asked myself dozens, maybe hundreds, of questions to help me know what I knew about our relationship that I hadn't known I knew.

As I asked more questions of myself, it became clear to me that the most productive use for this time was to learn more about myself. How did I or didn't I participate in the relationship? How had I contributed to the problems we now faced? If we chose to go on together, how would I participate differently in the future? What would that require of me? How would I know when I had fallen into an old relationship trance that no longer served me? How would I measure my success? Because we had no contact with each other, to use the time well I was forced to focus on myself and my role in the relationship.

The relationship with my former partner ended, but I was much richer for the process. I understood as never before how I had created exactly what I had feared in the relationship. I have come to believe that it really mattered little whether or not the relationship continued after our time out. What was truly valuable was the process that allowed us to know ourselves better and to better prepare us to be in future relationships. (Someone who has just lost a job, or feels threatened by termination, might do well to engage in such a soul-searching dialogue, farming what they "do not know" to learn more about their relationship with their job and their work.)

Not long after the relationship sabbatical, during which I had learned to hold myself in long-term deeply personal not-knowing, a member of a client group watched me sustain a group in not-knowing. What I am guessing was maybe 15 or 20 minutes of silence seemed like a long time to him. In the debriefing, he commented on watching me and said, "You're good—really good!" I thought to myself, "If you only knew what I'd been through to learn to do this!" But the work of mining our not-knowing and learning patience and comfort with silence in one area of our lives without fail affects all areas of our lives.

Ultimately, our courage is needed most as we give up being victims and, maybe for the first time in our lives, gain the inner power to live consciously, leaving behind old patterns. It has been said that we get a lot of mileage out of being a victim. In fact, as Dacher said, it has "street value." Many who play the victim role don't even realize it, but every time we blame something, someone, or a condition, or make excuses, we choose to be a victim. Market conditions change. New legislation is passed. A key employee quits. A vendor doesn't give good service. Until we discover our Magician, on some level, most people see themselves as victims. When we transform our relationship with fear, we are rewarded with the inner power to redefine what the circumstances of our lives mean in a way that allows us to move toward our fears, learning and growing every step of the way. When we transform our relationship with fear, we shed the role of the victim.

What Gets in the Way of Acknowledging Fear

We have thousands of excuses for not dealing with our fears, but the bottom line is that most of us are so emotionally incompetent that we don't really want to acknowledge and work with them. We are afraid of the power that comes from being awake. We are afraid of going into our not-knowing to learn a new way to be in our lives, our work, and our relationships.

Three out of four employees are trauma survivors.[3] When we have been hurt, especially hurt badly or at a young age, we are predisposed to be fearful. Such trauma contributes to creating many of our trances. So, although our fears ostensibly may be about what is happening in the workplace now, more often than not it is an autopilot response triggered by something that happened decades ago.

Ellie is the manager of a small work unit, which was plagued with difficulties when she assumed responsibility for it. We began working together because she was about to be relieved of her duties due to her apparent inability to generate any change. As we talked, she had a lot of good ideas about how to improve the unit, but she hadn't tried any of them. These new approaches to the work hadn't been tried in the company, and she didn't think her boss would approve. "Have you talked with your boss?" I asked. She hadn't. She had been afraid to bring up the ideas.

After a soul-searching session, Ellie and I discovered that she had always been told as a young girl that her ideas were dumb and she shouldn't think: she should just do as she was told and she would stay out of trouble. Subconsciously, this old trance programming from her childhood was driving her actions 25 years later! She still thought her ideas were dumb, and her programming had prevented her from ever trying them out. In fact, some of her ideas were very good, and they are now helping transform the work unit. Had she not consciously gone into not-knowing with me and challenged the assumption on which her trances were based, she probably would have been fired or at the very least demoted—and the company would still have a problem work unit.

Blaming also keeps us from consciously owning up to and examining our fears. When we blame, we take circumstances out of our control and choose to be a victim. We don't do this consciously, but we do it regularly. If we imply that conditions are beyond our control, why would we need to learn from our fears? Actually, learning from our fears robs us of being a victim and shows us that we can make a difference.

We even may contrive excuses to blame others for not being able to work with our fears consciously, relieving us of responsibility for going into not-knowing. Even if our organizational culture will not support a group process around our fears, those who strive toward emotional competence and living consciously will seek out those of like mind for an informal process or will simply do it on their own. What they won't do is say, "It would be nice if we could do something like that here, but we can't because . . ." When we blame, we can sound like we are awake, but we are really letting the "blaming others" trance prevail in our lives.

Acceptance without Accommodation

As individuals and groups of individuals begin to awaken from their trances, some will do so with more enthusiasm than others. For example, when I started waking up, I knew this was how I wanted to live my life, and I wanted to leave behind life in a fear-driven trance. Some around me were ahead of me in my personal growth work, and they provided encouragement. Others were about where I was, and we supported each other in our mutual quest for living consciously. However, still others were quite comfortable in their trance states. They didn't want to wake up—and they didn't want me to wake up either.

Emotional competence is about accepting where we are, accepting where others are, and respecting and honoring both of those places. An extremely challenging balancing act is demanded when we're with others who want to be in a trance state and to respect that *but* to not allow ourselves to be sucked back into our own autopilot trance. Of all the possibilities, it is without doubt the most challenging place to be. To be judgmental about other people's choice to remain in a trance is fairly easy and fairly common, but when we do that we are not holding up our own end of emotional competence by accepting and respecting them. To just throw in the towel, say it is too hard to be awake in a world of people sleepwalking through life, and just slip back into our own trances also are fairly easy and fairly common. To remain awake *and* nonjudgmental is much harder.

When we choose to accept others without accommodating their needs for us not to change, we face our own external motivation trance head on. We honor our own growth and our own choice to be on a path of consciousness, knowing it is right for us. Our judgment that others should change is an attempt to shift the external motivation system to one that coincides with our new life choice. If everyone is awake, our trance subconsciously says to us, then we don't have to worry about either their judgment about us or our accommodating their own life choice. But, that isn't how it works. That kind of thinking is still based on what others think, and it reflects the part of emotional incompetence that has to do with self-acceptance.

Any time we embark upon organizational change, resistance will emanate from those who are uncomfortable with the chaos and not-knowing that inevitably accompany change. We should not expect anything different as we begin to see the importance of emotionally healthy workplaces and start building emotional competence in them. As we do that, it is essential for us to remember that emotional competence means that we respect the position of others in their own growth and development. We must do that even when that includes their denial of fear and resistance to participating in group processes designed to cultivate an emotionally healthy environment.

No one should ever be made to feel that he or she must share his or her innermost fears until and unless he or she is ready to do so. This may happen early on for some individuals, and it may never happen for others. As we accept their resistance and provide a respectful space for others to share, over time as they see how important the information becomes to the group's work, even the most reluctant will generally begin joining the process.

I remember one three-day retreat I facilitated a few years ago, during which one woman didn't say a single word in our group process, but about midday in the second day, she began stopping to talk with me on her way out of the room for breaks. "This is really important work," she would say, but then failed to contribute. When the same group met for their annual retreat the next year, she actually joined in a few times, and by the third year, she was an active participant.

When we create respectful space for growing toward the process of transforming fear and developing emotional competence, even the most reticent will usually join in. If we try to force participation, we signal to those individuals that we do not respect them and their feelings. Our coercion is a red flag that this isn't a safe place in which to explore feelings, and those who were already fearful of taking part will have had their fears justified.

It is equally important, however, that we do not stop the process of developing emotional competence because one or two people are frightened by it. (They will not say they are afraid, because they are not in touch with their feelings. Usually, they will say something like, "This is not appropriate for a business setting," or "We don't have time for this. We have work to do," or something similar designed to distract others from their fear.) If we had decided not to go ahead in the retreat setting, the restrained woman never would have had the opportunity to become comfortable acknowledging her own emotions, and the rest of the group would not have had the opportunity to move forward in developing their own individual and collective emotional competence.

Impatience seems to be a normal condition of life today, and when we decide to do something we want to "Just do it!" Transforming fear is the teacher of patience. We will not do it overnight, or in a week or even a year. We do it, moment by moment by moment, by becoming conscious of our fears and using them to help us grow and move forward.

Looking Outside Ourselves for Approval

Emotional competence demands that we listen, ask questions, and accept what others are feeling, *even if it is not what* we *feel*. (Maybe even especially if it is not what we feel, because that is when we open ourselves to learn.) In fact, emotional competence acknowledges that, as human beings with different life experiences, it would be rather unusual for us to feel the same. Furthermore, emotional competence embraces both the diversity of feelings and experiences we have had and what we can learn from our differences when we accept that we think and feel differently.

If we are to develop a conscious strategy for learning from our fears, we also need to be keenly aware of the tendency most of us have to live our lives driven by externally motivated guesswork about what others will think about us. Trying to look good to others is the source of many of our autopilot trances. We want to be liked. We want to be accepted and included. We want to know that we are OK, but instead of looking inside of ourselves to see if we are OK, we look to the world. The world is doing the same thing. So, my trances reflect the trances of others, which in turn reflect back my own trance, creating layer on layer of make-believe between us.

We validate our thoughts by what we think others think. We validate our feelings by what we think others feel. We validate our hopes and dreams by what others tell us we should want. Unfortunately, it isn't the *real* others that are validating us but masks they have assumed because that is what they expect we want to hear from them. We live in a make-believe world in which we all think and feel the same, which is what we have believed we *should* think and feel. If individuals are awake enough to express what truly is real to them, most of our trances will quickly try to "fix" them by projecting our trance on them or intellectualizing away their fear. "Don't be silly. There's nothing to be afraid of," or "That wouldn't be possible. We have a backup system in place." We want to have the answer. We don't want to go into not-knowing.

When we deny another's feelings, we build an environment in which people shutdown and keep their feelings inside. Richard Barrett, founder of the Spiritual Unfoldment Society at the World Bank, says people then drift into meaningless responses. He says that when people say, "I'm fine," they are really using an acronym: Feelings Inside Not Expressed.

Our trances are quite comfortable with "I'm fine." We say it. Others say it. Nobody thinks about it. Nobody takes time to check inside to see how they really are.

We deny others true feelings, and by so doing, we deny our own—we deny our fear of acknowledging their fear. We resist the chaos that comes from discovering that everyone may not see the world as we do. We resist the chaos that may come when we search our souls and discover that we don't see the world the way we *should* see it—the way we think others want us to see it. We resist the chaos that results when we have the courage to say we think or feel differently than our perception of what others think and feel. We resist the not-knowing that comes from the chaos if we have the courage to sustain it.

For us to learn to work with fear, we must forsake allowing ourselves to be externally motivated. As long as we are playing a role that we think others expect, we will be in a trance. To work with our fear, we must be awake and in touch with what we as unique individuals are feeling and thinking that may not be in step with the rest of the world or even with one other person, and we must be OK with that. Instead of saying, "I'm fine," we must be awake to what is inside of us, without regard for what the rest of the world is saying. We must own up to it, and, if it has an impact on our work, we must share it. We cannot even begin to develop emotional competence until we can accept that what we hear inside of ourselves is OK. Until we do that, we will always be looking for someone else to blame for the way we feel. We begin to gain our power only when we listen to, accept, and honor ourselves as we are.

Lack of confidence is pretty common, even when it masquerades as arrogance. An important function of talking about what we fear is that it allows us to discover we share many fears. Instead of sitting around trying to guess what others are thinking and feeling, emotional competence gives us the tools to talk about what's on our minds and in our hearts.

The management group that failed to prevent disaster in the implementation of new technology, discussed earlier in this book, is a good example of this. In the Monday-morning quarterbacking session, each admitted that he or she had had one or more fears about moving forward. As we develop emotional competence, we can prevent these expensive disasters by voicing our fears before they become reality.

When we allow ourselves to be validated only by others, we will project that externally motivated system onto others. If we cannot honor the learning that may come from our personal fears, then we will never truly honor what comes from the fears of others. If we are subconsciously trying to "fix" ourselves by changing how we feel, we will try to "fix" others and change how they feel. In the process, we deny all of us the learning that comes from deep honesty and authenticity.

Transforming the Fear

- Magic appears to be mysterious, but it is really learning a set of steps and tips to do something and practicing until we develop confidence and skill to perform the "trick" consistently. So it is with the alchemy of fear. It is learning a set of steps to begin developing emotional competence, simple determination, willingness to make mistakes, and practice.
- Each of us has an ego whose purpose is to help us survive and a spirit whose purpose is to help us grow. Learning something new always causes tension between the two. This conflict may ensue for minutes or years as we develop confidence and practice at what we are wanting to become.
- The "granddaddy of all fears," the one at the core of most of our others, is the fear that we won't survive.

- By peeling away the layers of fears, we make it possible to make peace with the worst case scenario. When we have discovered how we can survive, and maybe even do well, within the worst case outcome, we free ourselves to fully participate in whatever we are doing.
- Asking questions about our fears brings them to consciousness and rationality and allows us access to our not-knowing to discover what we really *do* know but *didn't know we knew.*
- The "secret" ingredients to developing emotional competence are

  Awareness

  Consciousness

  Commitment to make learning a discipline

  Courage

8

Making It Happen

"We can learn to soar only in direct proportion to our determination to rise above the doubt and transcend the limitations."

. . . DAVID MCNALLY, *Even Eagles Need a Push*

The most powerful thing we can do in life is acknowledge, name, and accept our fear. Until we have done that, we will always be victims—victims of some unknown and unacknowledged bogeyman. Rather than step up to our own power to influence our circumstances, we will always be looking for someone, something, or some circumstance to blame. When we acknowledge our fear, we have regained the driver's seat in our own lives. By the very act of naming it, we begin to know what we must change in our own thoughts, speech, and actions to disempower the fear.

This process cannot even begin until we become aware of what is our current worldview, as represented by our habitual trances. Only by doing so can we come to understand that what we have considered to be an objective reality really is only one of many possibilities. Our trance states have been defining our world. We cannot know how our autopilot worldview formulates our perceptions of everything in that world until we know what it is. If we will consciously become aware of habitual behaviors and patterns of speech, they will help us identify our trances.

It is much easier to start this process in a group, where we can receive and give feedback and where everyone is looking consciously for trances. In our normal daily lives, our trances dictate almost every move we make. When we first are in the discovery process, it is difficult to know when we are awake and when we are in trances without feedback from others. It is not impossible to do this work alone, just much more difficult. This is likely to be the biggest life change that we will make, and respectful, loving support assists us in this major transformation.

If this is part of a group process, I begin by asking individuals to identify for themselves things that they know they do predictably—things they do or say without thinking. Later, I have them share those behaviors or patterns of speech with others in a small group. Next, I have others in the group give the person feedback about things they observe the individual doing in a predictable or habitual way. Finally, I have those same individuals share their personal reactions to the identified habitual behaviors.

Generally, the individual discovers that his or her colleagues have learned to "tune out" the trance-generated, habitual behavior. The individuals who consistently point to the impact on the bottom line, the employees, or the customers learn that their comments about these issues, although near and dear to them, generate a responsive trance in others. For example, if whatever topic is presented, Helen immediately starts asking, "How much is it going to cost?" her trance state is talking. The responsive trance that likely is triggered in her colleagues' heads may be, "Oh, there goes Helen again on her bottom line thing." Rather than really paying attention to Helen, they react with their own "ignore" or "dismiss" trance. This is disconcerting for most individuals to discover, but the discovery usually provides important

Group Trance Identification Process

1. *Self-awareness.* Each person identifies his or her perceived trances—the things he or she says and does predictably, "without thinking."

2. *Group awareness.* Members of the group give feedback to each other, identifying behaviors or language they perceive to be trance behavior.

3. *Responsive trance discovery.* Members identify their own response trances to identified trance behaviors and language. Members use this to gain group self-discovery about their effectiveness when operating in trances.

4. *Conscious behavior.* The group members identify ways in which they can begin to be more conscious about both their own behavior and language and their reactions to the behavior and language of others.

data indicating that the world, as they have experienced it, may not be how it really is.

Performing the Process Alone

Even though it is easier to learn to bring our fears and their trances into consciousness as part of the group process, it definitely can be done alone. If you will be working individually, you will need to involve friends and family in the process, which can present some challenges. The process will require more discipline, because it can be very time-consuming, and you may not like what you will be hearing. Unless those around you are reasonably emotionally competent, you may encounter significant denial, because simply inquiring about your trances will begin to make others aware of their own—something they may not be ready to do. The result may be responses like "That's not a problem," "I don't think you

Common Trances Used by Managers

- We (or I) don't know enough.
- I'll play "devils' advocate."
- How much will it cost?
- What about the people?
- Where's the data?
- "_____ study says" or "(expert) says _____ so we can't (or must) do it."
- It's not on the agenda.
- It's not in the budget.
- We lack the staff to do it.
- It's not realistic.
- It's just not possible.
- I don't know how we could ...
- I just don't know.
- That would never work (or never work here).
- You just don't understand.
- We did that before, and it didn't work.
- We've never done it that way before.
- If it ain't broke, don't fix it.
- If it ain't broke, break it.
- I'll be the "rescuer" and figure out how to keep people away from volatile issues or their feelings.
- I'll play "Little Mary Sunshine" and look for the bright side.
- Excitable "Let's do it!" Quickly jump on every bandwagon.

do that," "I haven't noticed anything like that," "I like that about you—that's part of who you are!" Remember that your predictability allows them to relate to you from their own trances. If you change, they no longer can trust their trances to get them through interactions with you.

Second, those who are unfamiliar with the concepts and terminology may not understand what you are looking for and sincerely may not be able to help. You may encounter a number of blind alleys, and once again you need discipline to keep at the task even when it is going slowly.

Finally, as you begin to do your work and start to be more awake about your own behaviors, often you will want others around you to do the same. They may not be ready. Emotional competence requires that you accept and respect the position of others. This can be very tempting, sometimes almost irresistibly so, but proselytizing can be damaging to relationships.

Just as in a group process, if you are working alone, you should begin by trying to identify those things you say and do so predictably that you do them without thinking. You may want to carry a little notebook for a few days to record your habitual patterns. These patterns may occur during work time, home and family time, recreational time, and during other activities that you regularly participate in, such as church or community affairs.

Next, begin asking those who know you well what things you say or do so predictably and regularly that they know what to expect before you do it. Ask them especially to help you identify "hot buttons" or things that they know will generate a strong reaction from you, positive or negative. Also ask them how they react or feel when you act in these predictable ways. If they like it, it may simply mean that they feel secure in knowing what to expect. It doesn't mean that it isn't a fear-generated trance, instead they may have their own trance reaction to yours. This is a common occurrence.

Start to ask yourself, "What causes me to do that?" Answers like "I've always done it that way," "That's the way I am," or "That's the way my mother did it" don't count. If you chose a behavior because it worked in your family system, you did so because you wanted to fit in. This is normal. The important questions to ask are "Is that really the way I want to do it?" "Is that really me?" "What would happen if I did something different?" "What am I afraid of?" "Is fear driving my behavior in any way?"

Then, engage in a period of "doing something different." As you begin to be aware of your trances, consciously choose to do something you wouldn't ordinarily do. If you always order vanilla, order strawberry. If you always take Main Street home, choose a back road instead. If your role in meetings is that of "devil's advocate," choose to consciously look for the strengths in another's proposal. What do you notice when you are doing something different that you missed while in your trance? What do you notice about how others react to you when you "do something different"?

Finally, some kind of personal encouragement system is useful to remind us that we are making progress. A daily success journal in which we enter the times that we acted consciously during that day will keep a more balanced perspective when we "slip" and become impatient with ourselves. A statement you say to yourself whenever you "slip" that reminds you how well you are doing and what a short time (compared to your whole life) you have been working on this can be most helpful.

If you are able to identify places where your trances cause you the most trouble, you may want to develop benchmarks, such as "I will relate with Susie consciously about her inattention to details one-half of the time." You may have normally reacted with an inner voice of judgment that said, "Can't she get anything right?" or by flying off the handle and losing your temper at her. This time share with her how her inattention to details affects you and how you feel about that. Sit and consciously develop a strategy for working together more effectively. Ask for what you want instead of assuming it is impossible.

Oddly enough, for most of us, it is easier to aim at one-half than to try to be perfect in the beginning, but just setting a percentage brings all of our interactions with Susie into consciousness. Each time you notice your inner voice of judgment, consciously choose to take the initiative to act consciously and

Individual Trance Identification Process

- *Identify people in different areas of your life who will help you with the process.* Explain to them what trances are and have them begin watching for things you say and do so predictably that they know what to expect. Don't offer them feedback on their own trances or in any way expect them to engage in the transformation process unless they choose to do so on their own.

- *Begin a program of self-awareness.* Keep a log of things you say and do so predictably that you do them without thinking. Notice how work trances vary from home trances and how both of those may be different than social trances.

- *Ask those who have agreed to help you for feedback.* Ask them about trance behavior (what you say and do so predictably they know what to expect) and your "hot buttons" (those things that others say or do that produce a strong reaction from you, either positive or negative) and to share with you honestly how they react to your various trances.

- *Begin to identify the source of trance behaviors.* Ask yourself, "Why am I choosing this behavior *now*?" Develop a conscious plan for breaking one or two of the trances you find to be most troubling.

- *Begin breaking all your trances by choosing to do "something different" in different areas of your life that have been dominated by habit.* Take a different way home, order a different kind of food than you usually do in a restaurant, choose to play a different role in meetings.

- *Develop a personal encouragement system.* Use it as a reminder that you are new at conscious living; keep a journal of successes, benchmarks for your progress.

differently. This usually means that we will far exceed our target, and it will allow us to experience success even when we slip into trance.

Initiating Change Gradually

Few of us can change multiple deeply ingrained behavior patterns at the same time. As a consequence, when I am working with groups on developing consciousness of trance states, I next ask the individuals to select one trance they want to concentrate on changing. Then, we can begin the deeper work of discovering what lies behind that trance. An exercise that peels away layers of intertwined fear and desire almost always will take the individuals simultaneously to both their deepest fear in relation to that trance and what they must change in their relationship to the world to regain their power in this arena.

So, for example, if Helen always is concerned about the bottom line, we may discover layers that relate first to the financial success of this particular initiative, next to the financial health of the company, on to her job security, then to the financial stability of her family and maybe even issues about old age and retirement, and finally to her ability to physically survive in this world. She may discover that her impassioned speech about the financial success of this new product line only in some small way is about this initiative, but underlying this trance response is a deep fear that she will not be able to survive in this world. Not surprisingly, Helen finds the granddaddy of fear—survival—is at the core of her fears.

When Helen discovers that survival issues drive her trance reaction, coming to trust that, whatever the outcome of the project involved, she will be able to survive and perhaps thrive will enhance her ability to participate fully at work. She will quickly discover that she can be less risk aversive at work and more supportive in leading-edge initiatives.

Rather than seeing herself as a victim dependent on the fortunes of the company, Helen begins to see herself as what Tom Payne has called a "company of one,"[1] an individual who is like an independent operator or business within the business. The "company of one" carries the personal security needed to participate fully in the workplace because the individual comes to know that he or she owns a skill set that will be valued outside his or her current place of employment.

Coming to know that her real fear is for survival opens Helen to knowing how she can take responsibility for her own survival rather than depend on her employer for it. This shift in thinking allows Helen to reclaim her personal power, which she has given over to the enterprise. When she is free of the yoke of her fear, she can break out of her way of going on automatic pilot in meetings and other workplace interactions. She is free to consciously engage in dialogue about new initiatives. Rather than spout the same lines she always has, she can participate in openly exploring new ideas in a way that builds the group intelligence about the proposal. She still can ask questions that will explore the financial impact of the project. But when she is fully awake, she also will want to know about company values, purpose, market position, consumer demand, and quality. This is the power of identifying her trance state and naming her fear.

Those working individually can do something similar.

Select the particular trance pattern that, if you changed, would benefit you most in life. (If you need help, you may want to review the list of "Common Trances Used by Managers" appearing in this chapter.) Begin looking at what fears are associated with this trance. You initially may believe there are no fears, but ask yourself a series of probing questions that will take you deeper into understanding your trance.

Something as simple as taking a back road home may produce a response like, "I'm afraid of wasting the extra 10 minutes." That doesn't seem like such a big deal on the surface. But, as you probe deeper, you may discover more about your relationship with time, family members, and yourself. "Why is 10 minutes so important to me?" "What difference would it make if we had dinner at 6:10 instead of 6:00?" "What would happen if I am 10 minutes late to my meeting?" "What difference would driving by the park make to my temperament when I get home?" Each of these invites still deeper questions, which may point to fear of disapproval of others, fear of negative judgment, or issues around personal self-worth.

Other trances may affect your life more integrally. If, for instance, you are the devil's advocate, who always looks for the downside or the negative aspect in any situation, what do you fear that causes you to react in this way? "What would happen if I chose to look for the credibility in the proposal or idea?" "What do I miss in life by being so negative?" "What makes it so important to me to be judged competent or analytical?" "What impact does my negativity have on the people in my life?" "If I always react negatively, how do people know when a problem is really serious?" Oftentimes, such hypervigilance was born in childhood out of a need to receive approval from a parent or teacher who was equally critical. The need has long since passed, but the trance continues to drive your life to the discomfort of family and friends.

We regain our personal power when we begin to realize that the world as we have known it is only an illusion largely defined by fear-induced trances. When we see ourselves as dependent on our employer for life-and-death survival, we limit how fully we can participate in the life of that enterprise, and by so doing, we withhold information from its collective intelligence. Our trance-induced efforts to support the survival of the organization then actually undermine its success, because we are subconsciously choosing not to put all we know into its collective intelligence.

When they are named and honored, fears become tools for group learning about a situation, an issue, or elements of an impending decision. They thereby improve the quality of decisions, ease of implementation, responsibility for a course of action, the relationships of parties involved, and the general climate surrounding any action. Furthermore, because more data emerge and decision making is more thorough, meetings have a more relaxed and committed tone, and a higher standard of truth surfaces.

The Time Factor

The process may feel cumbersome, awkward, and even give the appearance of being time consuming in the beginning. Our knee-jerk concern about time is a common trance and largely a function of the concept of time as limited and linear. This concept of "mono-chronic" time suggests both that we can only work on one thing at a time and that we are not working on something if somehow we aren't tangibly giving it attention.

Those who have worked in Asian and Hispanic cultures are likely to have experienced a different concept of time—"poly-chronic" time. Polychronic time suggests that we are working in many time dimensions at once, and we may be actively working on a project or several projects when we appear to be doing something completely different.

Frequently, when stuck on a problem, I take a break and go for a run or a walk. Suddenly the answer is there. I appeared not to be working on the problem, but a different part of my brain, in a different time dimension if you will, was still working away while I was running.

This polychronic phenomena is characteristic of many of the processes I have described in this book—cocreating in community, working on our fears, and demonstrating our emotional competence. It may seem that we are "off on a tangent," talking about something unrelated to the topic at hand, as we work on someone's fear, anger, or sense of loss. Often, however, when we turn back to the subject, a quantum leap has occurred in our thinking. While we were focusing on our emotions, we were free-ing mental capacities that had been consumed with keeping down our emotions to more fully explore the topic at hand. When we return to "work," often major strides occur in our under-standing of our production system, marketing plan, research focus, or whatever other else is "the order of business."

Whenever we are learning to do something new, the task will take more time than when we are experienced at it. Over time, we will develop a facility for consciousness that will become almost as easy as our autopilot modes have been, except that we will be awake. During the transition, it is important to consider that these processes are understood more easily in relation to polychronic time. Although our concentration must be total and focused on breaking our trances and facing our fears, in another dimension, we are cultivating our mental field for the business at hand. Over time, we will develop the ability to integrate emotional competence and the order of business so well that the process will be enjoyable and work easily with little thought or effort.

Emotions or Emotionality

That emotions can either propel us in the direction we choose or impede our ability to achieve our mission has long been discussed, but many people have confused learning consciously from our emotions with emotionality. Both emotionality and fear of facing it are signs of emotional incompetence. When we don't accept our own emotions as legitimate indicators of something that needs attention, we tend to stifle them until, like an overloaded powder keg with the right spark, they explode in emotionality.

We've all had the experience of saying or doing something that seemed pretty benign and having someone "overreact." Most frequently, a momentary surprise is coupled by a quick internal "won't do *that* again." To this day, I remember having a boss explode at me over 25 years ago. His face and balding head turned beet red as he screamed to me about not doing something. I hardly knew what hit me, but I didn't want it to happen again. Later, he discovered that he had failed to give me the task in question. Although he apologized, there was a significant level of fear in all of my interactions with him thereafter.

Now that I have developed a level of emotional competence, I realize that his explosion was only a little bit about me and what I had or hadn't done. It was a great deal more about him and accumulated fears he had about being perceived as incompetent by his superiors.

Perhaps a more common kind of explosion occurs in bosses who want to fire someone. Often after months of unsatisfactory performance, an employee will do something that the boss interprets as "the last straw." However, the boss has never given the employee a clue that his or her performance was unsatisfactory. The boss kept putting off addressing the problems, all the time loading his or her emotional powder keg. The last straw is usually not a "hanging offense," but because of the accumulation of offenses, it becomes one. A manager's fear of confrontation with an employee often leads him or her to ignore performance issues that should be addressed *as they occur*, preventing the build-up of emotion.

If we are emotionally competent, we are comfortable sharing our emotions as they develop, rather than invalidating them so they fester, ready to explode, sometimes with the slightest trigger. When an "explosion" does occur, we recognize it as an overreaction that probably had little to do with the apparent source of it. We honestly acknowledge that the reason for it was a long-term build-up produced by the failure to deal with emotions when we first felt them.

Our emotional incompetence is further displayed in how we react to the emotionality of others. Those who are emotionally competent know that an overreaction is caused by a build-up of unprocessed emotions. They are not afraid of the other individual's reaction because they understand it, so they don't "get sucked in" to their own fear of the reaction. They can be present, accepting, and respectful—and reflect the other's response in a way that creates a safe space to explore what is going on. This might look like something as simple as, "You really seem to be angry about what happened here. Let's talk about it."

The emotional competent then has the wisdom to listen to both the words that are being said and the nonverbal cues. They may respectfully and inquisitively ask for examples and details, accepting what the other individual feels *even if they do not agree* or would not have felt that way themselves. A statement like "I can see how you might feel that way" accepts the feelings of the other, without projecting how he or she might have felt differently. The ultimate goal of the emotional competent is to engage in deep listening without trying to fix, change, or invalidate what the other is saying, thereby providing a safe environment for exploring emotions.

Most leaders and managers are as emotionally incompetent as any of us in our lack of understanding of emotions and emotionality. They steer clear of the emotional component of our interactions, out of fear of losing control. That only leads to even more suppressed emotions, emotionality, and failure to recognize this important data source. A specific approach designed to help us develop emotional competence in the workplace has been totally lacking.

Transforming the Fear

- Our trances define our world and our limitations. The process of overcoming our fears cannot begin until we are aware what our worldview is and that it is just one of many possibilities, rather than objective reality.
- Although it is easier to learn to bring our fears and their trances into consciousness as a part of a group, it can be done alone.
- Few of us can change multiple deeply ingrained behavior patterns at the same time. Change is more manageable and more effective if we choose one or two trances that have the most impact on our lives and concentrate on changing them. When we have developed more conscious behavior patterns in those areas, we can choose others to work on.
- We often think that we don't have time for "process" work such as working with fears. Time is not an objective reality. It is one way to view the world and will be colored by our own trances.
- Most of us think of time as linear and limited. Work on emotional competence and cocreation in community func-

tion best in polychronic time, which suggests we may be functioning in many time dimensions simultaneously.

- Many people confuse emotions with emotionality. Emotionality results from neglected emotions that become like dynamite in a powder keg, waiting for the right spark to set off an explosion.
- Emotional competence demands dealing with emotions as they are experienced, preventing the storage of feelings and the volatility that results.

Could It Be Love?

9

"Our deepest fear is not that we are inadequate. Our deepest fear is that we are powerful beyond measure. It is our light, not our darkness, that most frightens us. . . . We were born to manifest the glory of God within us. It's not just in some of us; it's in everyone. And as we let our own light shine, we unconsciously give other people permission to do the same. As we are liberated from our own fear, our presence automatically liberates others."

. . . NELSON MANDELA, quoting Marianne Williamson
in his 1994 Inaugural Speech

It has been said that there are really only two emotions: love and fear. From this perspective, all the upside emotions—joy, peace, enthusiasm, trust, satisfaction, happiness and so on—are some manifestation of love. All the downside emotions—anger, sadness, loss, frustration, humiliation, irritation, confusion, and so on—are some manifestation of fear. Because I spend a lot more time working with people who are in the downside, I can say that it has certainly been my experience that whenever we probe any of their downside emotions, we invariably end up with some kind of fear.

My own personal experience with the upside emotions validates the theory that love is the basis for all of them but perhaps with a qualifier. The love that is at the core of joy, peace, enthusiasm, trust, and all the others is an unconditional, universal love that spiritually connects us all through time and space. Time as we have known it stops. A deep resonate peaceful energy seems to flow through us when we feel this kind of love. It is peaceful. It is joyful. It brings us to life with enthusiasm. We discover faith and trust.

Love Is What It Is All About

Suppose there were a secret instruction book for life that none of us knew about when we came into this world, and because we didn't know about it, we have just been trying to figure what to do as we went along. We haven't known what to do. In its desperation to ensure survival, our egos have focused on what threatened us as we muddled through life. So, life has been frightening, and we haven't been doing very well. Then, suddenly one day, we find the instruction book, and it says:

- Love is what life is about.
- Love is what work is about. It is a place where we can unconditionally provide love and support to many people. It is a place where we can unconditionally receive love and support from many people.
- Our purpose in life and work is to *be* love and bring more love into being.

Interesting prospect, isn't it? Love has been the other four-letter word that we have been afraid to talk about at work. Oh, occasionally it comes up, but usually being confused for lust, in the context of sexual harassment or the office romance and as something to be avoided. Unconditional love? Being love? Creating love? As the purpose for our work? Never. Don't let the words cross your lips in most workplaces.

That's just not how it has been. Regardless of what is said, if you watch what goes on in most workplaces, in fact, in most of the world, you would believe that we all had received an instruction book that said:

- Fear is what life is about.
- Fear is what work is about. It is a place where we should perpetuate fear in any way we can. We should do unto others before they do unto us.
- Our purpose in life and in work is to be fear and bring more fear into being.

How might we approach our lives and our work differently if we discovered we had accidentally received the wrong instructions? The trances that carry us through most of our days are the product of fear, yet love can be experienced only when we are being fully conscious. So, we clearly would have to start being fully awake in life. We also would have to start being intentional about every act in which we engage. We would need to consciously ask ourselves, "Since my purpose in this action is to create love, what will I do? If I am to reflect my true being as love, what will I say or do right now?" We would spend a lot more time in not-knowing. We would have to choose to be mindful of each word we say and each act we perform to make sure that it creates more love.

The Fear and Love Paradoxes

In *Leading from the Heart*, I described the phenomena in which the closer to Spirit we get, the more aware we become that much of life exists in paradox. Love and fear both present us with paradoxes with which to live. First, the fear paradox, which I discussed in depth in *Leading from the Heart* and mentioned earlier in this book, is that, when we are afraid, we take actions that cause us to create the very thing we fear. If we are afraid that we cannot create workplaces full of love, then we will never have loving work-

---

Fear and Love Paradoxes

Fear paradox. When we are afraid, we will take actions that will create what we fear.

Love paradox. If we love conditionally, it is because we are afraid we won't get certain things that are important to us. Because we are acting from fear, we *won't* get them. If we love unconditionally, we are more likely to get the things we might want from a relationship, but we cannot love *in order to get them* (loving conditionally) or we will not get them.

---

places. We won't have them because we cannot create them, we will not have them because we never tried.

Unconditional love creates its own paradox. By definition, when we love unconditionally, we do so without the expectation of getting anything in return. *Anything.* We don't love others to get them to love us in return or else what we are doing is neither love nor unconditional. We can't love others to have a better-run business or it isn't unconditional. By the very definition, we cannot expect *anything* or it becomes conditional, and that isn't love.

When we love unconditionally, generally others *will* love us in return. The pure heart is difficult to resist loving. When we love unconditionally, generally we *will* have a better-run business. Love invites openness, honesty, accountability, responsibility, and sharing of fears that hold important teachings, creating an environment that naturally invites effectiveness. Herein lies the paradox, if we love unconditionally we will get the things we might want, but we cannot love *in order to get them* or we will not get them.

The love paradox closely relates to the fear paradox. As the fear paradox tells us, when we are afraid we will create what we fear. So, when we love conditionally, it is because we are afraid we won't get certain things that are important to us. Because we are acting from fear, we *won't* get them.

Creating an Environment for Love to Flourish In

For our organizations to survive in the future, we must begin to see our work first as building an environment in which love can flourish. When we see our organizations existing to create power in every person through the power of love, we will see empowerment. But we cannot experience love at work until we experience love in life. My perennially favorite definition of love is Scott Peck's from *The Road Less Traveled*. He defines love as "The will to extend one's self for the purpose of nurturing one's own or another's spiritual growth."[2]

If we are to know love in life or in work, we must be prepared to extend ourselves, even far beyond our comfort zones, for our own spiritual growth and for that of others. The spiritual work we have to do is to create an environment in which love will flourish. We do whatever is needed to help ourselves and others wake up, name our fears, especially the "granddaddy," and reclaim our power for being responsible and intentional about what we create.

At a professional meeting a few months ago, a young woman told a story of reclaiming both personal and organizational power through the transformation of fear. At her company's annual strategic planning sessions, tension emerged. But it seemed apparent to participants that what they were arguing about wasn't what they were arguing about. Something was going on under the table.

Finally, it came out. The owner and CEO of this socially responsible corporation felt burned out. He needed a break and wanted a sabbatical to pursue other interests. However, he was afraid that, if he weren't around to champion the values on which he had built the company, it would fall into what has become "business as usual" in most of the United States.

Members of the management team were afraid as well. He was an essential driving force in their company, not only because he so vigilantly advanced the values but because he made a significant contribution to the thoughtfulness with which the company did business. When some of the fears finally made it to the table, real dialogue could begin to address them.

The group decided to adjourn, and each member went to a quiet space. Each was to reflect on the fears he or she had about the proposed transition. When they reconvened, they shared their individual fears, and much to their delight, the fears held a lot in common. Eventually, they were able to develop a strategy for allowing the CEO to take a sabbatical, addressing all their concerns, and building deep connection on the team that had never before existed.

The young lady that told the story had tears running down her face as she talked about their process and the emotional bond that they had created as they built a plan that allowed all of them to achieve their hopes and dreams. They extended themselves to nurture their CEO's growth and, by so doing, nurtured the growth of everyone in the room. And, they tapped the power of love at work.

Despite the personal, emotional, and spiritual imperative to repeatedly engage in this ultimate act of love, an organizational effectiveness imperative is included as well. When we are locked into a survival mentality by our fears, we preclude access to our rational brains. As this young woman's story demonstrates so dramatically, when we bring our fears to consciousness, understand, and honor them, we open ourselves to effectively use our rational brains. The pace of change is too fast and the stakes too high today to make our decisions while on automatic pilot. We can no longer make our decisions without full access to part of our brains, excluding important information from consideration because of our fear of bringing it to consciousness.

Uncomfortable Questions

When I reflected on "What are we afraid of?" what immediately popped into my mind was "Could it be love?" Could we be afraid of living a life full of love? Could we be afraid of giving this universal love to everyone we came in contact with unconditionally? Could we be afraid of receiving love unconditionally? Could we be afraid of loving ourselves enough to build workplaces bereft of fear? Could we be afraid of loving our work? Could we be afraid of our power when we are living fully consciously? Could we be afraid of living from what Mandela called "the glory of God within us"?

A client once said to me, "You ask the most uncomfortable questions." I do. My job is to awaken people from their trances, so I ask questions that take them to their not-knowing in order to challenge how they have believed the world had to be. Even if it is just for a brief moment, there will never be the surety in their resignation that was there before. There will never be the certainty in their blaming and being a victim. So, I ask uncomfortable questions. Could we be afraid of love?

To imagine living in a world in which we gave and received love unconditionally, we loved ourselves unconditionally and without limits, and we manifested the glory of God within us takes most of us deep into not-knowing. Not-knowing is a place we resist because if we come to know something fundamentally different about our world, we would have to make fundamental changes in how we relate to that world. We are afraid that we won't be able to do it. Most of us haven't articulated it, but from all I have been able to observe, I can believe only that we are afraid we won't be able to relate in a world filled with love. So, we choose fear. We have trances that get us through a fearful world. We have no trances for a world filled with love. Love is awake.

After my client groups describe their legendary organizations in great detail, I ask them, "What would you personally have to do differently to be in this legendary organization?" I now ask similarly uncomfortable questions about living in a world of love. "What would *you personally* have to do differently to be in a world filled with love? What would *you personally* have to do differently to work in a workplace filled with love? What would it look like if *you personally* manifested the glory of God within you in all that you do in your life?"

I always follow the "What would you personally have to do . . ." question with another, "What would it take for you to be willing to commit to doing that?" Now, I ask you, "What would it take for *you* to be willing to commit to doing what you've said you would need to do to live in a world filled with love?"

These are critical questions, and they are at the core of creating meaningful organizational change. We have been accustomed to asking fearful questions: "How do we avoid . . . ? How can we protect . . . ? How do we ensure . . . ?" We have little experience determining what our responsibility is for creating love. We cannot and will not have effective or spirit-respecting organizations until each one of us is willing to look at these uncomfortable questions. And, we need to hang out with them in not-knowing long enough to discover the deep resonate peaceful energy that flows through us and tells us that we can do it, we must do it, and each one of us is the only one who can make it happen.

Being in Love

When most of us think of "being in love," we think of the somewhat debilitating, lusty, lightheadedness romanticized by Hollywood and song writers. Cupid proverbially pulls back his bow and lets loose with an arrow to our hearts and that of another. We get all puffed up, lose our appetites, and there is magic in the air before we "live happily ever after."

There is another kind of "being in love," and it is the other kind that I am writing about here. It is being in a state that transcends our normal human ego and the usual experience ego drives in our lives. It is connecting with the human spirit that takes us into the flow of universal love.

By nature, the ego is fearful. Its function is to help us physically survive in the world. It relishes in fight or flight because that's how it knows to survive. For the ego, it is a dog-eat-dog world, and we've each got to do whatever it takes to survive. Individual ego fears have exploded into collective organizational fears built on the belief that it is a dog-eat-dog world, and they pervade virtually everything that we do at work.

The self is the part of us that is the "glory of God within us." It is deeply spiritual. It is the source of faith, trust, and confidence that things will work out. It knows we are all connected. It understands and thrives on cocreation in community. It knows that help will always come when we allow it and often in strange and mysterious ways that our ego could not begin to predict or understand.

When I talk about being in love, what I am talking about is dropping into the spiritual place of one's self and tapping the great universal love we find there.

"I Want to Be in Love"

I recently attended a work session of organizational professionals dedicated to understanding the relationship between spirit and leadership. Within an hour, the two-sided themes of love and fear began bubbling forth, so integrally are they related to living and working in ways that nurture the human spirit.

One woman shared her personal struggle to figure out who she was once she ripped away all that her ego had led her to believe she was. "When all that's not me is washed away in the great nothingness, I want to be . . ." she hesitated, "in love." It was apparent from the universal and instantaneous agreement from all corners of the room that this woman had articulated so eloquently what we had all been coming to know but had yet to verbalize. We all wanted to be in love—everywhere. Especially, we wanted to be in love at work. Not the lusty Hollywood version of love. What we wanted was to be in love with the divine nature in all of us and to work from that place. We wanted to do what Mandela says "We were born" to do: we wanted to "manifest the glory of God within us."

The same group devoted significant reflection on how we transform our fears. As many shared their own personal experiences in changing their relationship to fear, their themes clustered in two categories:

- Talk about fears, bring them to consciousness, get them on the table and in the light
- Do something that connects you individually or as a group to something bigger, something divine.

When Mandela spoke to the light within us, I believe he spoke of this universal love that is the human manifestation of the divine nature in each of us. Love is the light. It is conscious, fully awake, fully present. Fear is the darkness. It is the absence of the divine and love. We begin the alchemical process when we bring fear into the light, when we bring it into the light of love. It cannot survive in its consciousless ego state in the presence of the light of love. That is why it is absolutely critical to bring our fears to consciousness and to articulate them.

Likewise, the power of tapping into universal divine love drowns fear as we have known it and, with a new perspective, allows it to be reborn in a friendly, useful way. Some spoke of prayer, others meditation, or forms of meditation like keeping journals and breathing deeply. One talked about walking in nature. Another spoke of consciously reviewing similar circumstances in her life with gratitude so she came to see the hand of the divine in everything that she experienced. All of these are ways in which we are able to tap into whatever is "bigger than we are," and find peace, faith, trust, and consciousness. They are ways that we can "shed light"—the light of love—on whatever we fear, gain insight and understanding about it, and discover new confident ways of moving forward with our fears instead of being held back by them.

Changing Our Relationship with Time

When we are being love at work, just as when we are being love in life, our very being is different than it has been when we are being in fear. Our relationship with time is one that drives much of what we do, far beyond what any logic can imagine. Driven by the little things of life, we neglect the important things on which the little things depend, usually because our trances have us fear that we haven't enough time. Love is able to listen, be patient, and be open because it isn't "afraid we don't have time for that." Love knows that we don't have time *not* to listen.

It never fails to astound me the total lack of logic that our trances have when it comes to the perception of time. We don't consciously build relationships before we sign contracts with major contractors or customers because "we don't have time." We don't consciously build a relationship before we enter joint ventures or mergers because "we don't have time." We don't adequately train employees because "we don't have time." Yet the very same people who give me these explanations will complain about how much time and money they are spending cleaning up the fallout of not having done these things.

Six hours spent in building a relationship between partners in a potential merger convinced both parties that it was "not a marriage made in heaven." They were able to shake hands, wish each other well, and agree that they would both be happier in a partnership embodying more aligned values structures. They would have spent more time than that just pulling together the legal paperwork for the deal, yet most companies would not have done it because they would be afraid they didn't have the time.

Conversely, a friend of mine is working on a project that is way overdue because parties cannot agree on what needs to be done, but "we don't have time" to get together and air all of their interests and agree on a common vision for the project.

Love listens. Love is patient. Love is not afraid to put "the important ahead of the urgent," as Stephen Covey would say.[3] Love knows where its priorities are and isn't afraid to stick to them, regardless of how attractive the fear-driven distractions of the day may be.

Love also is open and respectful. Consequently, it is with some trepidation that I mention prayer in connection with tapping into our divine nature at work, lest some zealot choose to impose group prayer on others. If we are to love and respect our coworkers, we must recognize that many paths lead to the divine, and we must show deference to the different ways in which each of us chooses to pray. I would never lead a group prayer anywhere but in a group affiliated with a particular religion, and I would discourage others from doing it as well. I often ask people to take a few deep breaths and spend a few minutes in silence, connecting with their core self. Some may choose to pray to a divine source outside of themselves. Others may choose to connect to their own inner divine source. I don't know, and I don't care. What I do know is that after such periods of silence, ego-driven differences and fears can be addressed from a place of love, and incredible clarity and even unity emerges. They have discovered what it means to be love at work.

Why Is Love So Frightening?

Like any of our fears, our fear of love can be transformed from a generator of trance-driven avoidance into a wise and friendly teacher only when we articulate what we fear. So, why is love so frightening? Although people have a number of fears about creating love at work, they generally fall into three categories, each of which will give us critical insights into what we have to do to create love and simultaneously address the concerns about which the fears are to teach us.

The most common reaction to this topic is "I would do it if everyone else would." If we're waiting for others, it isn't unconditional love at all. Furthermore, the category of fears represented by this statement is fear of vulnerability and abandonment. When we bring love to work, we are open, honest, responsible, and accountable. We give up playing politics and games. "But, if I give up the games and politics, people will take advantage of me." Love doesn't care. Love is unconditional, but it isn't wishy-washy. Because love begins with self-love, we don't let people steamroller us.

We do need to discover new ways to relate to people that are open, honest, and loving and that are self-respecting as well. That may mean addressing issues directly with people instead of gossiping through a third party. It may mean asking directly for information instead of playing trading games to get it. There are no rules. We simply must ask ourselves as we go along, "How will I handle this to create love? How will I handle this if I love myself? How will I handle this if I love everyone involved?" The answers are not easy. They require us to be mindful, conscious, and intentional about all we do, and they will inevitably require us to go into not-knowing for long periods or engage others in cocreation to arrive at a loving resolution.

Organizational vulnerability also concerns potential sexual harassment litigation, about which every employer seems to be frightened. Sexual harassment is not love. Love is respectful, honoring, and accepting of others feelings. Love listens. Love is conscious. Sexual harassment is none of these. Sexual harassment is born of the worst trance state material. It is not respectful, self-respecting, honoring, accepting, listening, or conscious. Love cannot tolerate sexual harassment. If we want to bring more love to our workplaces, we certainly would want to be even more vigilant about stopping the trances that give rise to sexual harassment than ever. Deep dialogue into the meaning of love will shine a light on the difference and help participants appreciate on a spiritual level what is and is not appropriate in a way that a legalistic approach will never do.

The second category of fears relate to approval issues. Here are some statements typical of those afraid of having others judge them negatively:

"There's a lot of sharks here. That would be pretty wussy!"

"I don't know what to do. I might make a fool of myself."

"I'd do it, but others wouldn't trust me. They'd think I was just playing another game."

"We don't have time for that kind of stuff. We have work to do."

These fears call upon us to use an externally motivated guidance system rather than an internal one. In our hearts we know what we want to do is bring more love into our lives and into our world. When we listen to our inner guidance, we know what we need to do. We simply need to connect with that place in us that is OK being who we truly are, that place where we love and respect ourselves enough to do what we know is right.

The third category of fears relates to lack of faith and might be called the *fear of failure*. Actually, both of the other categories of fears might justifiably be included here as well, but because they are more frequently articulated I wanted to treat them separately.

Quite frankly, our greatest fear of bringing more love to our workplaces (and for that matter our lives) is that we're afraid we won't be able to do it. For most of us, we simply don't know how to love unconditionally. We don't know how to love ourselves, and we cannot even begin to think about loving others until we can love ourselves. We don't believe in ourselves and our ability to love, so we cannot believe in the ability of others to love. We spend so much of our lives in trances that we cannot conceive what it might be like to sustain conscious loving. And, perhaps ultimately, we are afraid that if we discover what it feels like to live love and not be able to sustain it, we won't be able to stand the pain of going back to a fear-driven life. So, our fear of failing keeps us from ever trying. Our fear creates what we fear the most: our fear of not being able to love keeps us from trying to love, so we don't.

One More Fear

Well, I guess there really is one more fear, but it is the most frightening to talk about so I am speaking to it separately. Our deepest fear is the one Mandela addressed, our fear that "we are powerful beyond measure" when we are living love. For a culture addicted to being victims, the prospect of power terrorizes us. Peaceful, loving, mutually respectful power that each of us experience as so abundant and bountiful that we don't have to worry about losing it to others or taking it from others is just plain frightening. Or, maybe it is magic—the magic of alchemy that occurs when we choose to turn our workplace fears into workplace love.

Creating Love

Creating love is not like instituting statistical process controls with a clear set of rules that are quantifiable and measurable. We have no clear-cut way of knowing if it is happening or isn't happening, except that if we are open to receiving love, we know it is there because we either feel it or don't. It cannot be a "program" to be implemented. It cannot be forced or required. Creating love is largely a moment-by-moment, conscious decision-making process because we want it with all of our being. As so often is the case when we live from our hearts, souls, spirits, or whatever term one wants to use to mean the essential part of us, we are guided much better by questions that help us understand the nature of unconditional love at work and in our lives than we are by rules.

The exact wording of the questions we use is less important than that they take us consciously, in present time, into not-knowing and cause us to thrash around there for however long it takes to find an answer that spells L-O-V-E. The questions need to ensure that we are not in anyway acting from fear, so some should expressly address that. Questions already presented in this chapter, such as those in the box on the next page, that cause us to create a scenario of what it would look like if we were creating love in this particular situation, may be useful. Questions that ask us whether any unspoken conditions are attached to the love we give may help. Questions that challenge our assumptions about what we know about both love and work can be insightful.

Being fully awake and asking questions simultaneously helps us sustain a workplace built on love and makes us aware of when we are acting from fear, but some cocreating in community is helpful in getting the process started. The group will want

---

Questions to Guide Definition of Workplace Love

- When we have a workplace full of love, what will be happening? What won't be happening? (Look for dozens of details.)

- What will it look like? What will we *see* happening? What *won't we see* happening? How will people *talk* with each other? What will we *hear*? What *won't we hear*?

- What will alert us that we may be putting conditions on love? What will alert us that we may be back in our trances?

- What will tell us if our decisions are in any way motivated by fear instead of love?

- How will we measure our success? How won't we measure our success? How will individual success be measured?

- What will we do to develop capabilities that we currently lack?

- What will be our relationships to ourselves in order to create more love? What will be our relationships to each other? What will be our relationships to our work? What will be our relationships to the world outside our organization?

- What do we fear? What does that tell us? What will we do to both address the concern presented by the fear and create more love?

- What problems could be created by a workplace full of love? What can we do to consciously plan for those problems before they occur? What will we do when problems we aren't able to plan for occur so that we don't react in fear when they happen?

- What can we do to support each other as we learn to create more love?

- What will each of us individually need to do consistently to create what we have described? Are you willing to commit to doing that? What does commitment mean to you?

---

to spend a significant amount of time "drawing the blueprint" for what it wants to create, and the blueprint will be different in every organization. We don't do this work so that it can be "implemented" but to afford everyone who cares the opportunity of going collectively into not-knowing to discover what each will come to know he or she must do. You may have questions of your own to add, but answering the questions in the box will provide you a clear set of guidelines from which to work.

After this work has been completed, a similar set of sessions should address where the organization currently is and how we must change our relationships and our systems to bridge the gap. This most definitely should include examination of all workplace rules, policies, and procedures to determine which ones support a workplace of love and which ones are built on fear. Some may need to be eliminated and others reworked. Some may not need to be changed at all, but the frame of mind and heart from which we administer them may change. The criteria for determining success for individuals, work units, and the whole organization likely will need adjusting.

(For those wanting to bring love to work on their own, a similar process can be done alone or with the help of a few like-minded friends.)

The paramount trait of a workplace built on love rather than fear is people who are awake, aware of their fears and their fear trances, and consciously choosing to act from love and not fear. Whatever can be done to create those characteristics inevitably will create more love. For this reason I reiterate that love at work cannot be treated as the latest trend from the Management-of-the-Month Club. It *cannot* be a program to be installed or implemented because such approaches, of necessity, are based on a premise that people won't get it if we don't tell them how. We *cannot* build workplace love on a fear-based premise.

Let There Be Peace on Earth, and Let It Begin with Me

I remember a hymn from my childhood that started, "Let there be peace on earth, and let it begin with me." All change starts within us individually. We cannot change the world. Each one of us can change only ourselves and how we individually relate to the world. Just like peace, love begins with me. And, it is by changing ourselves and how we relate to the world that we will change the world.

But, "It is our light, not our darkness, that most frightens us." Choosing to live consciously without the safety offered by our trance-induced blaming and excuses frightens us. Stepping off the cliff of being a regular human driven by fear, protected by trances, and safe in what we have believed we knew, stepping up to the fully awake "glory of God within us" frightens us.

For several years, I have given many new clients Robert Fisher's wonderful little book *A Knight in Rusty Armor* to help them as we begin our work. The story concerns the spiritual journey of a medieval knight. Toward the end of the book, the knight is struggling to climb The Summit of Truth. As he clings to the mountain, he notices an inscription chiseled on a boulder:

> Though this universe I own,
> I possess not a thing,
> for I cannot know the unknown
> if to the known I cling.[4]

Eventually, the knight realizes that he must let go of everything he believes he knows, including the boulder to which he is clinging, and he finds himself falling into the memories of his life.

> Faster and faster he dropped, giddy as his mind descended into his heart. Then, for the first time, he saw his life clearly, without judgment and without excuses. In that instant, he accepted full responsibility for his life, for the influence that people had on it, and for the events that had shaped it.
>
> From this moment on, he would no longer blame his mistakes and misfortunes on anyone or anything outside himself. The recognition that he was the cause, not the effect, gave him a new feeling of power. He was now unafraid.

As an unfamiliar sense of calm overtook him, a strange thing happened: he began to fall upward! Yes, impossible as it seemed, he was falling up, up out of the abyss! At the same time, he still felt connected to the deepest part of it—in fact, he felt connected to the very center of the earth. He continued falling higher and higher, knowing that he was joined to both heaven and earth.[5]

We have been hanging on so tightly to our belief in a fear-filled world that we have been unable to let go of that perception. We have been afraid to let go of what we knew and risk falling into the abyss of not-knowing. We've missed the experience of being "joined to both heaven and earth"[6]—the connection to something bigger than ourselves. We have been unable to create workplaces filled with love because we have been unwilling to let go of our fears of lost security, the judgment of others, vulnerability, and abandonment. And, no one else can do it. It is in each of us, and it must begin with each of us. It is only when "we let our own light shine, we unconsciously give other people permission to do the same."[7]

This is the alchemy of fear. It was miraculous for the knight, who discovered that when he let go of what he knew, let go of blaming, let go of everything outside of himself, he fell *up* to The Summit of Truth. Just as miraculously, when we are able to let go of our fear of love, we truly discover the capacity to love fully and unconditionally. When we have discovered it, others will discover it through us. The magic is in the acceptance that, as long as we are afraid of it, we cannot love. Fear and love cannot coexist. Letting go of fear as we have known it and learning to honor and love our fears transforms *us* into love. When we stop letting fear drive us, we stop thinking of love as something we have or possess, and we come to know that love is something we are. When we learn to love our fears and gratefully accept them for what they tell us, alchemy occurs, and *we* become love. And we discover our true inner power is the power of love.

Transforming the Fear

- There are only two emotions: love and fear.
- The trances that carry us through most of our days are the product of fear. Love can be experienced only when we are fully conscious.
- Fear is a paradox: when we are afraid, we will take actions that will cause us to create the very thing we fear.
- Love is a paradox: if we love unconditionally, we usually will get the things we want, but we cannot love in order to get them or we will not get them. When we love conditionally, it is because we are afraid we won't get certain things that are important to us. Because we are acting from fear, we won't get them.
- If we are to know love in life or work, we must extend ourselves, even far beyond our comfort zones, for our own spiritual growth and that of others. The spiritual work we have to do is to create an environment for love to flourish.
- We must be willing to ask uncomfortable questions about what it will take and what each of us is willing to commit to doing to create love.
- We have wanted to be in love with the divine nature in all of us and to work from that place.
- Fear cannot survive in its consciousless ego state in the presence of the light of love.
- Love is frightening to us because

  We fear vulnerability and abandonment.

  We fear negative judgment from others.

  We are afraid we can't do it—we don't know how to love either ourselves or others unconditionally.

  We are afraid of our power when we are living love.

- Creating love is a moment-by-moment, conscious decision-making process that asks, "If I want to create love with all my being, how will I act in this particular situation?"

- The paramount trait of a workplace built on love rather than fear is people who are awake, aware of their fears and their fear trances, and consciously choosing to act from love and not from fear.
- When we let go of our fear of love, we will discover the capacity to love fully and unconditionally.

10

The Act of Love

> "Mental toughness is humility, simplicity, spartanism, and one other . . . love. I don't necessarily have to like my associates but as a man, I must love them. Love is loyalty; love is teamwork. Love respects the dignity of the individual."
>
> . . . VINCE LOMBARDI

Love and fear cannot coexist. We may go from one to the other in a matter of seconds, but we cannot sustain universal, unconditional love and be afraid at the same moment. The ultimate act of love must be to change our relationship to fear: to bring the light of consciousness to our fears and to love them as wise teachers and friends. By so doing, we bring love and all that it has the power to create into our individual lives and into our organizations.

We cannot, nor should we try, to erase fears. Fears will always be with us and for good reason. They are the product of the ego, and they are intended to teach us how to prepare and what to avoid in order to survive. They bring us important data to help us survive individually and organizationally. They are not there to stop us, but instead to lovingly remind us of what may need attention. When we learn to love them, we are still able to survive, but we are liberated from the survival mentality, where all we can do is survive. If we want to thrive in work and in life, we must discover the love to move us through the fear that holds us in survival thinking.

As I discussed in Chapter Seven, awareness is the first step in the process of transforming our fear. To some extent, survival issues can be found in everything we do. As a consequence, an element of fear is involved in every task of living. Most of us have learned to move through our fears of the normal activities of living, so that we do them without thinking. This is where our trances serve us. Although there are some who would say we should be fully conscious of our every movement, that exceeds the purpose of this book. However, as we become aware of when we are going into trances, we can choose when to let them serve us.

If we really thought about moving down a highway at 70 miles per hour surrounded by a thin piece of metal and plastic and dozens of drivers who are drunk, angry, sleepy, or otherwise at less than an optimal level of function, also driving 70 miles per hour in thin pieces of metal and plastic, we might be reticent to jump onto the freeway. In fact, when we were first learning to drive, we may have actually experienced physical queasiness during our first solo venture on the interstate highway system. And, some people still experience debilitating phobias of the most essential functions of our daily existence, such as regularly driving to work.

We could not function in daily life if we had to consciously think about everything we do and all the possible fears that might be related to what we do. Yet, because these activities have been reduced to trance behavior, we often neglect to bring to consciousness related fears that might serve us. When we have had too much alcohol to drink or a heated argument that keeps us from being completely present in our driving, we might be well served to bring our fear of driving to such a state of consciousness.

But, instead of choosing when we will go into trances, we anesthetize ourselves from all our fears in a continuous trance so that we lose access to their important information. We probably all know people who have been involved in motor vehicle accidents because they weren't completely alert to the demands of driving. A coworker who was distracted thinking about an equipment problem at work and a friend whose husband had just had a heart attack were in accidents that each credited to "not thinking about what I was doing."

More often than not, however, we are limited in our effectiveness not because of fears that we have learned to accept and move beyond, but those we have failed to recognize, articulate, understand, and learn from. If we have not brought them to consciousness, they cannot be our teacher and friend. They certainly cannot be a wise guide offering us confidence, conviction, commitment, and courage. They have not and cannot be transformed because we don't know they are there.

More Power of the Question

We have talked about the power of asking questions to take us into our not-knowing, challenging our assumptions about both what we know and what we don't know. Perhaps the most damaging assumption that we make in our work and in our lives is that we aren't afraid. Yet, fear is everywhere around us, and for good purpose. Our trance-induced assumption that we aren't afraid is robbing us, and the only way that we can wake up to our stolen power is to ask assumption-challenging questions. When we ask the powerful question, "What are we afraid of?" we immediately take ourselves to our not-knowing and learn what might otherwise have been missed. We don't ask, "Are we afraid?" to which we could give a quick trance-induced "No." We assume the fear is there, availing us of the opportunity to learn.

Peeling the Layers of Our Fears

We tend to give circumstantial responses to the "What are we afraid of?" question. "We're afraid we are going to lose market share to ABC Company if we don't beat them to market with this new product." Those fears are important teachers about the situation or problem at hand. They help us be more effective managers. However, if we stop with this question, we may miss some of the most important learning. It is essential to remember that facing our fears is like peeling an onion: the fears always are layered and the core holds the whole thing together. It is important to know that more layers always lie underneath. As we develop our emotional competence, we come to understand that the ones at the core are those that paralyze us or surface as counterproductive activities.

When we have fully explored what we believe the fears are, if we once again ask a question that invites us to go into not-knowing, we will discover more fears. I hesitate to prescribe an order of questioning because what works for one topic may not for another. However, when I am working with groups, two dimensions motivate the questions that I ask: breadth and depth.

"What else are we afraid of?" is built on the assumption that there are multiple fears, and we are trying to identify all of them. It invites broad discovery. The company that was afraid of losing its market share may also discover that it is concerned about quality, adequate time to plan a marketing campaign, or lack of training for service personnel if the product comes to market too soon. Each of these teaches us something important about the decision.

At the same time, however, deeper fears impede our action. I find that repeatedly asking the same question, allowing for dialogue each time, leads both individuals and groups to their deeper fears. Following the identification of the initial fear, I would repeatedly ask, "And, if that happened, what would we be afraid of then?" So, for example, after the company afraid of losing market share had discussed and learned about that fear, the managers would ask, "If we lost market share, what would we be afraid of then?" This sequence tends to take us into our personal fears by identifying what keeps us from throwing ourselves into this project 100 percent. It helps us make peace with the worst-case scenario so once again we can free ourselves to participate fully in our work. When we know we can survive the worst, there is no longer reason to hold back our best. We are free to excel individually and collectively.

What Does It Look Like?

Any decision-making process needs to inquire into the fears that may hold important information to be considered. Major initiatives, like new product releases, may require several sessions to adequately address everything that needs to be in the new product action plan. Such a process can get very complicated, and to reproduce the dialogue involved would require a lot of space and could jeopardize confidentiality agreements with my clients. However, for readers to experience just a sampling of what it might look like, I am sharing a grossly simplified, generic, and totally fictional conversation that might have occurred around a new product launch in a fast-growing company similar to many with whom I work.

Stan, Alma, Ruth, Rick, and Ellen are five members of the management team of Do Everything Software Company. They have been learning to transform their fears and want to be fully conscious in their deliberations about marketing their new software package, Do Everything Again. Each of these managers has fears relating to the launch that he or she has not been accustomed to thinking of as fears. Stan begins their process by asking, "What are we afraid of?"

Ruth, the sales and marketing manager, is pressing the team to move quickly. She has heard that their main competitor, Us Too, is working on a program that will compete with Do Everything Again. She feels it is important to be the first in the market with this product so theirs will be used to define the niche. The market is so hungry for this product that she is afraid that, if Us Too beats Do Everything to market, it will capture a huge segment of the market instantly, as well as establish the industry standard.

"So, if that happens," Ellen asks, "what would we be afraid of then?"

"No one would buy our product," answers Alma.

"So, if that happens," Ellen asks again, "what would we be afraid of then?"

"This is a tight business. If we aren't producing state-of-the-art products, we won't be around very long." Ruth responds. "I'm afraid we will go out of business, and I personally have a significant financial investment in the company in addition to having worked 60-hour weeks since we opened our doors."

"So what are you afraid of, Ruth?" Stan asks.

This time becoming very quiet, Ruth notices her voice crack as she answers, "Everything will go down the drain. It will all have been for nothing." The rest of the team is quiet while they reflect on their emotional competence work.

Finally, Ellen says, "Ruth, I know that you have been working very hard, and it would be an awful waste to lose it all."

Tears streaming down her cheeks, Ruth chokes, "I didn't realize how much the demands of this job had gotten to me. I've been doing it because I believed in this company—not just the product, but the way we have agreed to work together. So much is at stake."

Stan asks again, "Ruth, you sound like you are at the end of your rope. We've been learning that when we are afraid, we create what we fear. So, what are you afraid of?"

"The financial loss would create a significant hardship for my family, and I feel that they have really suffered while I have been working so many hours. But, I guess what really frightens me is the thought of having to go to work in an 'ordinary company' again. What we have built here really feels good. I really enjoy going to work for the first time in my life. The thought of going back to a job that feels like drudgery is just too much."

"If our fears really do cause us to create what we fear, Ruth," Alma asks, "how could your fear lead you into a job that feels like drudgery again?"

Ruth is quiet. The others listen respectfully for two or three minutes. Finally, she answers, "I guess by pressing to market Do Everything Again before it is really ready. I remember the disasters we had when we came out with Do It All before we had the bugs worked out. That gave Us Too a chance to catch up with us in the first place."

Rick, the customer service manager, also has been concerned that the company avoid the problems experienced after the release of their premier line, Do It All. "That's something I've been afraid of," he adds in agreement.

"What does this fear have to teach us then?" Ellen asks.

Ruth is the first to speak up. "It teaches us to think things through and to do our homework. It also teaches us to pay attention to these things. I was just so panicked that Us Too was going to get to market before we did, that I wasn't even thinking about the disaster we might create if we got there before we were really ready."

The group continues to work on their fears, developing an action plan that will be implemented before they go to market with Do Everything Again. Each member of the team has important fears, which hold important information that can affect the successful launch of the product.

Ellen, the accounting manager, is concerned that inadequate study has been given to determining both the cost of goods sold and the cost of properly marketing the product. Furthermore, cash flow problems have been pervasive in recent months, and she is concerned that the company can't generate the capital to launch the new product.

Stan, the human resource director, has concerns as well. Increased production will necessitate increasing the number of employees by one-third. This will require hiring and training management, production, and service personnel. Another software firm in their small community just increased production and has hired a significant number of new employees, leaving a dearth of good workers in their labor market. Currently, Stan is a one-man show in HR, and he is worried that he will not be able to deliver the people required to staff the project. He feels that the company will have to increase wages to attract the people they need. That causes additional apprehension for Ellen and her cash-flow problems.

Alma, manager of research and development, knows the product still has serious problems. Her department is feeling pressured to deliver before all the bugs have been worked out of the product. She is afraid that if a disaster occurs, her department will be blamed.

At the end of the process, the team has a good action plan of what needs to be done to bring Do Everything Again to market so everyone will be proud, and the company will prosper. In reflecting about the process, Ruth observed, "You know if we had done this before we introduced Do It All, we may not have ever heard of Us Too! I feel really good about this. I feel like we are all pulling in the same direction now, instead of being at odds. We all want the same thing for the company. I realize now how easy it is to feel like we are disagreeing when we don't talk about the real issues."

Stan, Alma, Ruth, Rick, and Ellen have been creating love at work, and they have done it by performing alchemy on their fears. They have taken what appeared to be divisiveness and transformed it into connection and a coalesced strategy for moving forward in harmony.

More Consciousness Brings More Love and More Confidence

The dialogue between the managers of Do Everything Software of necessity was simplified but should give readers a tangible example on which to build. A group that was experienced at working with their fears would want to spend much more time and develop a great deal more detail about how to address their fears.

Some of the Fears Identified about Reorganizing and Merging Two Departments

What is the fear?	What will we do to address it?
"We won't have adequate time or staff."	Regularly assess what we are doing. Ask critical questions frequently: • What can we do differently? • Do we need to do this? • Who else does it? • Who might do it more easily? • Have we involved others? • Have we mapped the process to determine what might be creating the task?
"We won't really be able to make it happen."	Involve all the staff in mapping the tasks that need to be performed and how they relate. Have patience with ourselves and each other. Have realistic expectations about what can be done and how long it will take. Put together a deliberate plan with timelines that are realistic and people are committed to meeting. Build in scheduled process checks. Remember that slower is faster—to do things right will take time and involvement. Remember that when people are involved, they won't let it die. Have everyone take responsibility for ensuring the success. Celebrate successes as we go along.
Resistance by people in each department to sharing information and work they previously "owned."	Involve everyone from the beginning. Get them involved in identifying what needs to be shared. All managers should be clear that there is no territorialism between them. Spend time in personally working with each other. Challenge any statements that divide us.

Whatever we do to shed more light on our fears will give us more power over them. Our power is in the consciousness we have about them.

For a new product start-up like the one in which Do Everything was engaged, a helpful strategy would be to develop a map of the whole system that graphically, as well as verbally, represents how each different department must interact with others and on what timeline. At each juncture, the group would want to ask, "What will we be afraid of at this point?" Then a specific plan can be developed to ensure that fears have been addressed. Every time we let go of even the most insignificant of fears, we make space for more love. We also build confidence that we will be able to accomplish what we planned, allowing us to bond through the power of love rather than through our powerlessness.

Being in Love in Our Personal Relationships

Perhaps, we are most likely to think about being in love in our personal primary relationships, but too often these are built on a superstructure of fear, just like our work relationships. The granddaddy is at work here, too. In my individual coaching, I regularly find the people gripped by fear of losing their jobs are equally frightened of losing their primary relationship. Somehow people do the same thing with their personal relationships that they have done with their jobs—they have come to believe that they cannot survive without them. Similarly, they haven't been able to fully be part of those relationships because they haven't discovered the freedom to survive without them.

Once again, this is not rationality at work. This is primitive fear, but fear keeps people from being fully a part of their primary relationships. They talk about needing more alone time, but they are afraid to talk with their partner about it. They talk about wanting to do important service work, but they are afraid their partner doesn't get to see them enough now. They talk about wanting to learn to paint, or sculpt, or dance, but are afraid to talk about that, too. They may even talk of needing a different job, but are afraid the family can't survive financially if they follow their hearts. Instead, they lose their aliveness and live their relationships in a comatose state that is disconnecting at best. They have been so needy for the relationship that they have been afraid to be fully who they are within it. They have not been in love in the relationship; they have been in fear.

All people are different, so all reactions are different, but when I am able to get people to share their hopes and dreams with their partners, magic often happens. Sometimes, they even discover their partner has similar desires that have gone unexpressed. When someone has the courage to talk about his or her hopes and dreams, it can provide a safe atmosphere for a partner to talk about what he or she wants as well. They discover love and new life in the relationships.

I once worked with a couple who had owned a business together for many years. For most of the time, she had been quite unhappy with what she was doing and had a personal passion she had longed to pursue. When she finally shared both her displeasure at what she was doing and her desire to pursue her passion, her husband was shocked. "Why didn't you tell me?" he said. He immediately followed with encouragement that they could work together to make the transition from her job and into what she wanted to do. She, too, was shocked. Trapped in a job she had hated for years, she had been separated from her dream by only a few sentences—and her fear of saying them.

Creating Love

I know something about love. I know more about fear and courage. I certainly have not mastered any of them. I am simply a normal person on a path to experience life more fully and joyfully. In the process, I have discovered that the most profound way in which we can bring more love into our lives is to be aware of our fears, name them, face them, learn from them, and move toward them. I am not exactly sure how it works. But, I know that, when we perform that act of love, more love comes into our lives. I don't know if it creates space that has been consumed by the dominance of fear, if it opens a door through which love can enter, or if like mixing a recipe, it actually generates love where there has been none. I am not sure that it matters. If we are willing to go through the steps, alchemy will happen—we will turn fear into power, the power of love.

Transforming the Fear

- Love and fear cannot coexist. The ultimate act of love is to change our relationship to fear, bringing to it the light of consciousness and love.
- A great deal of power lies in asking the question "What are we afraid of?" When followed by "And, if that happened, what would you be afraid of?" the questions will take us deep into our core fears. This will allow us to make peace with our worst-case scenario, freeing us to fully participate in the work at hand.
- When we follow "What are we afraid of?" with the question "What else are we afraid of?" it will identify a broad spectrum of multiple fears.
- We can be fully part of a relationship only when we have discovered the freedom to live fully without it.
- The most profound way in which we can bring more love into our lives is by being aware of our fears, naming them, facing them, learning from them, and moving toward them.

11

The Power of Love

"Love is the highest, purest, most precious of all spiritual things. It will draw out from men their magnificent potential."

...ZIG ZIGLAR

History, for most of us, has concerned bonding with others through our powerlessness, wherever we have felt victimized. At work, we have bonded over what we thought were unfair situations: hours that were too long, vacations that weren't long enough, traveling on our days off, inadequate training, insufficient warning of and planning for change, downsizing, reengineering, foreign competition, new legislation, potential litigation, the grouchy boss. At home, we have bonded over jobs we didn't like but thought we had to do, spouses and children that didn't live their lives the way we thought they should, abusive and alcoholic parents, taxes we think are too high, and the neighbor's howling dog that keeps us awake at night. Shackled by real circumstances, societal expectations, our own sense of powerlessness, and others who reach out to share their own powerlessness with us, we have sought strength by bonding through our mutual powerlessness.

But it doesn't work. When we bond through our powerlessness, we simply reinforce our sense of being victims. We become more fearful. Our conversations regularly reinforce how hopeless it all seems. We fortify ourselves in a theme of us vs. them, and often "them" turns out to be the world as we perceive it, always harboring a bogeyman to fear and blame. Our fear of our powerlessness creates more powerlessness. We develop an emotional warfare mentality and clothe ourselves in armor that keeps captive our own power, just as it prevents others from reaching out to help us in love.

Fear breeds it all, but we don't talk about our fear. When we bond through powerlessness, we bind ourselves to our fears, and thanks to our protective trances, we do it without thinking. We do it because our trances have told us that is what we should do. We do it as individuals who complain to a friend about our children or spouse. We have done it as big business greedily gobbling up more and more subsidiaries because we think that will make us more secure, and then we do it by downsizing or reengineering from the top down. We do it as big labor, uniting workers against management. We do it as whole nations.

The now nearly defunct communist system is the most graphic example of the failure of bonding through powerlessness. The communist system was based on bonding through powerlessness, but powerlessness breeds powerlessness, fear, and trance behavior. Systems that guaranteed to take care of people, of necessity, created countries of dependents and codependents. Whole nations of people moved through life in trances, spiritually dead and robbed of hopes and dreams.

Other Paths to Spiritual Death

At the same time, much of the Western world is bound in another way. It is bound through a different approach to powerlessness. We have called it *rugged individualism* and *independence*, but what it amounts to is agreeing on a system where we are afraid to let go of control of even the most inconsequential conditions of our lives and work. If we can't predict, force, and control what outcomes will be, we are afraid of dire consequences. Then we freeze in inaction or lash out in reaction. We have bonded through a system that says we are safe only when we are independent and can control our circumstances. We have believed our security lies in predictability. We have blindly tried to believe in predictability, yet nothing is as predictable as change. We have put our security in organizations, conditions, and circumstances as they are now, pretending somehow that if we believed they would not change, they would not.

Although it has been less graphic than the demise of the communist system, the system that has revered independence, control, and predictability has produced countries of people living in trances, who likewise are spiritually dead and robbed of hopes and dreams. Any system built on fear eventually will lead us to the same situation—sleepwalking through life. Recent attempts to build more interdependent workplaces through teamwork and other forms of participatory management have sparked some life, but they have been superimposed on the old fear-based system motivated by its fear-based beliefs. Our evaluation and reward structures largely have continued to be based on the same framework. We have "pushed down decisions" but people, locked in trance by the "granddaddy," have been afraid to exercise authority for fear of being fired, and we haven't helped them find their power in personal entrepreneurship.

A Different Way

There is another way, and our relationship to fear makes the difference.

> A happy person is not a person in a certain set of circumstances, but rather a person with a certain set of attitudes.
>
> . . . HUGH DOWNS[1]

Just like a happy person is characterized by a set of attitudes, a person owning his or her full personal power is characterized by a belief structure with a different set of attitudes about what is real and what is possible. From the new belief structure, we bond through our hopes and dreams. We bond through our aliveness, creativity, and unique gifts. We bond through the power of love. Love is awake. Love is responsible. Love is intentional. Love is full of hopes, dreams, and possibility. When we bond through the power of love, we share our hopes and dreams, we come to know what is the responsibility of each person for cocreating those hopes and dreams, and we intentionally assume our responsibility. It is powerful. It is the power of love at work.

A colleague told me about work that is bringing life to one of the country's most crime-ridden inner-city housing projects, among people who have for centuries been bonded through their powerlessness. Junior high school-aged children have been trained to interview their neighbors about what they love in their neighborhood and what their hopes and dreams are. The age of the interviewers has freed those being interviewed to tell stories they have kept locked inside, and by so doing, they are reaching part of their souls that has laid dormant for much, if not all, of their lives. They are awakening each other to possibility and responsibility, and they are doing it through the power of love. They are helping their friends and neighbors bond through their hopes and dreams and not their powerlessness.

This has been missing from the "empowerment" movement in modern organizations. We have neglected the large-scale dialogue needed to shift our assumptions to ones based on love and to build systems that nurture our hopes and dreams. We have failed to provide the processes that will wake up people, so we all can work consciously. We have failed to help people discover the power of love and the magic it holds. And, we have failed to do it because we have been afraid.

The people on the management team who identified their fears about the president taking a sabbatical discovered the power of love at work. The wife who had the courage to tell her co-owner husband that she hated her job discovered the power of love both at work and at home. The owner who, after several attempts, finally learned to let the team make decisions discovered the power of love at work, and so did the team. The new product team at Do Everything Software learned the power of love at work. Individuals in each of these groups identified fears that separate them, and by bringing them to consciousness, they discovered the power of love in working together more effectively.

An End to Cheerio Lives

A colleague of mine talks about our "Cheerio lives," lives with a hole in the middle. Our work and lives, in general, have had a hole in the middle because we have sliced away much of our essence by denying our emotions. When we buried fear, we closed the container that holds all of our emotions. As a result, at a time when energy, enthusiasm, creativity, capability, courage, and joy are desperately needed in our organizations, they are unavailable to us. Not only are they unavailable to us, but without them, unnamed fear keeps us locked in inflexibility and without the resilience to respond to ever-changing conditions at work and in life.

The alchemy of fear is the first step in making our hole whole. It is the first step in developing emotional competence, which will allow us to live full lives. Fear in the closet is like a tiger behind the door. We're not talking about it, yet we are distracted from other work as we silently wonder what will happen when it comes out. We are unable to rationally address important issues in the here and now because we are locked in future time thinking about when it might get out. When we acknowledge that the tiger is in the closet, and we all are concerned, we can consciously develop approaches by which we can meet it on our terms, whenever it emerges. Then, with the confidence of being well prepared, we can turn our full attention to other business at hand.

When we begin to develop a competence at opening to fear, we also open ourselves to other emotions critical to our workplaces and lives. Emotional competence not only allows but encourages us to experience the power of love, as well as the energy and enthusiasm that inevitably accompany it, and to thrive in our work. Emotional competence enables us to experience peace in the not-knowing of chaos and thrive in the humdrum of "just grinding it out."

Real Empowerment

Emotional competence in relation to our fears finally offers us promise of bringing to life the empowerment we've been hearing about for years. Power in the language of "fight or flight" often is perceived as dark, manipulative, and coercive. It is power applied *against* another or others to gain something the ego believes it needs. It is the empty power of autocratic managers.

Power in the language of love is healing, supportive, and joyful. It is power from the inside out. Power gained from others is temporal—it will not last, and it demands constant recharging from external sources. Power generated by being whole within ourselves is self-regenerative. Having inner power generates more inner power. Changing our relationship to our emotions supercharges our inner power supply with love. That is where our security should rest. When we put our security outside our selves in organizations or people, we always will be fearful that it will be taken away. When our security rests in our own inner power supply, we know that we will never run out.

Emotional competence allows us to create more satisfying relationships and outcomes. We can be fully present for those with whom we work. We can be "real" with each other, because we needn't always fear others will discover a hidden part of us. We can be with our fear rather than become our fear. When we do this, we uncover the key to the creation of the circumstances of our lives and that is truly empowerment.

It is time for those who lead our organizations to develop the courage to be open to the potential power and capacity in our organizations by freeing fear, accepting all emotions as an essential component of everything we do at work, and opening to the power of love. The promise of energy, joy, creativity, and health that results from living and working in full consciousness is ours simply by making a commitment to developing the emotional competence of our organizations.

No longer is there a reason for emotional incompetence in the workplace—simply excuses. The tools are simple: awareness, consciousness, commitment, courage, and practice, practice, practice.

The Courage to Be

If we are to create an environment in which love can flourish, we can do it only through the boldest acts of personal courage and the power of love. To truly create love at work, we need to create a growth-rich environment and have both the courage and emotional competence to dwell in not-knowing long enough to discover what it means for us to be "in love" right now in this particular situation. That may occur in months or it may happen in the blink of an eye. We must have the courage to *be* with it—to sustain the not-knowing while we come to know what our responsibility will be and what will be required of us. That will happen only if we are fully awake, fully in touch with every part of ourselves, and have the emotional competence to *allow* it to happen in a society that wants to *make* things happen.

Sustaining the Tension

The most quintessentially spiritual thing that we can do is to hold ourselves in the mystery, what I have called the *not-knowing*, and open ourselves to learning. A constant tension stands between what we believed we knew and either the not-knowing or what we are coming to know that conflicts with what we believed we knew. The tension may never be greater than as we come to explore what it means to be in love at work.

Fear and love cannot coexist but they are in constant juxtaposition. They symbolize every existential dichotomy we face in life: the ego trying to survive vs. our divine essence striving to thrive, the practical, feet-on-the-ground, get-the-job-done part of us vs. the part of us that wants to soar with the eagles, resignation vs. embodiment of our hopes and dreams, the cynic vs. the idealist. We have been taught to choose between them, implying that there is a right and a wrong, but the alchemy lies in letting go of the need to know right or wrong and accepting that both are true. The magic is in choosing to have it all.

Some readers will reject my premise out of hand, saying "This is crazy!" Others will cheer, "It's about time!" But, the large majority of people will feel a tension as they read this very sentence. A part of us has been told that success lies in effectively performing a set of business competencies well—have the right product at the right time, market it right, keep costs under control, deliver high-quality products and you will succeed.

Yet, even that part knows that some part of everyone working that way is dead, just going through the motions of life. And, it wants to be alive. It beckons to the other part of us: it wants to be alive, it wants to be in love at work. The tension is there, and it will continue. The only answer is to learn to relate consciously to all that we do in a way that allows and encourages both to happen.

The Neverending Story

One of the most deeply spiritual films that I know is a children's film, *The Neverending Story*. It is required viewing for many of my clients, because it artfully portrays the tension between having our feet on the ground in order to get by in life and bringing the animating force of our hopes and dreams to life.

In the film, the Nothing is destroying Fantasia, the domain of human hopes and dreams. It creates the worst kind of destruction. It doesn't even leave a hole, because "that would be something." There is just nothingness. A great adventure story unfolds as the creature-hero Atreyu seeks to save Fantasia from the fast-encroaching Nothing. The kingdom will be saved only if a human child believes Fantasia can be saved.

The father of Bastian, the human child who holds the potential to save Fantasia, recently lectured him on the importance of "keeping your feet on the ground" and "getting on with your life" after the death of the boy's mother. While a part of Bastian wants to believe he can make the difference, he is reluctant because of his father's castigation. Just as the kingdom appears to be doomed, Bastian speaks the word that he must to salvage what remains of Fantasia, and by so doing opens himself to the magic of possibility. When he believes, he discovers that all his dreams come true.

The "never-ending story" is that through our hopes and dreams we are able to spawn the hopes and dreams of others, thereby starting a self-perpetuating cycle of belief.

So it is with being in love at work. When we believe we can make magic happen by waking up and transforming our fears into love in the workplace, we can do just that. And, we can fan the flickering hopes of others who believe there is a better way to work. The hope sleeps in each of our hearts and needs only to be awakened. The alchemy of our fear lies in simply allowing ourselves to discover the magical power of love within each of us. When we, like Bastian, are willing to let go of the cultural programming that has told us to be practical and keep our feet on the ground, we open ourselves and our workplaces to the love that requires us only to believe for the belief to become reality.

Transforming the Fear

- History for most of us has concerned bonding with others through powerlessness wherever we felt victimized. But this doesn't work. When we bond through powerlessness, we simply reinforce being victims, becoming more fearful. Our protective trances allow us to do this without thinking.
- Rugged individualism and independence are other ways that our trances bind us to our powerlessness and stop us from giving and receiving love.

- Any system built on fear eventually will lead us to the same situation—trance living.
- When we bond through our hopes and dreams, we bond through the power of love.
- Our work and lives have had a hole in the middle because we have sliced away much of our essence by denying our emotions. The alchemy of fear is the first step in making that hole whole. When we open to fear, we also open to other emotions critical to our workplaces.
- Power in the language of "fight or flight" is dark, manipulative, and coercive. Power in the language of love is healing, supportive, and joyful. It is power from the inside out and it will never run out.
- The promise of energy, joy, creativity, and health that results from living and working in full consciousness is ours simply by making a commitment to develop emotional competence in our organizations. The tools are awareness, consciousness, commitment, courage, and practice, practice, practice.
- In order to truly create love at work, we need a growth-rich environment, emotional competence, and courage to dwell in not-knowing long enough to discover what it means to be "in love" right now in this particular situation.
- There is a constant tension between what we have believed we knew and what we are coming to know that conflicts with what we believed we knew.

Notes

Chapter 1: Recovering from Organizational Brain Damage

1. M. Scott Peck, *Further Along the Road Less Traveled* (New York: Simon and Schuster, 1993), p. 23.
2. *Webster's II New Riverside University Dictionary* (Boston: The Riverside Publishing Co., 1984), p. 90.
3. Ibid.
4. Kay Gilley, *Leading from the Heart: Choosing Courage over Fear in the Workplace* (Boston: Butterworth-Heinemann, 1997).

Chapter 2: Facing Our Fears

1. Peck, *Further Along the Road Less Traveled*, p. 23.
2. Herman Bryant Maynard, Jr., and Susan E. Mehrtens, *The Fourth Wave —Business in the 21st Century* (San Francisco: Berrett-Kohler, 1993, 1996), pp. 38 and 80.
3. Jon Kabat-Zinn, *Full Catastrophe Living—Using the Wisdom of Your Body and Mind to Face Stress, Pain, and Illness* (New York: Delta Trade Paperbacks, 1990), p. 168.
4. Maynard and Mehrtens, *The Fourth Wave*, pp. 105 and 109.
5. Peter M. Senge, *The Fifth Discipline—The Art and Practice of the Learning Organization* (New York: Doubleday/Currency, 1990), pp. 16–26.
6. Ibid., pp. 24–25.
7. Daniel Goleman, "The New Thinking on Smarts," adapted from *Emotional Intelligence*, *USA Weekend* (September 8–10, 1995), p. 4.
8. Gilley, *Leading from the Heart*, chapter 13, "Avoiding Fear Creates What We Fear the Most," p. 190.

Chapter 3: Emotional Competence

1. Elliott Dacher, "Post-Modern Medicine: Expanding the Healing Model," keynote address at the Integrating Mind, Body and Spirit in Medical Practice conference, sponsored by Duke University, Chapel Hill, NC, October 5, 1996.
2. Kabat-Zinn, *Full Catastrophe Living*.

Chapter 4: Resisting Emotional Competence

1. Eleanor Roosevelt, "This 'n that," cited in *The Hope Heart Institute Newsletter*, vol. 4, no. 3 (Fall 1996), p. 8.
2. Dacher, "Post-Modern Medicine."
3. Caroline Myss, "Why People Don't Heal," an audiotaped lecture (Boulder, CO: Sounds True, Inc., 1994).
4. Ibid.
5. Kabat-Zinn, *Full Catastrophe Living*, p. 334.
6. As quoted in Valerie Brown, "Science: We Feel, Therefore We Are, Too,— Neurologist Antonio Damasio Lectures at the Hult," *Eugene* [Oregon] *Weekly* (September 28, 1995), p. 13.

Chapter 5: Chaos and the Fear of Not-Knowing

1. M. Mitchell Waldrop, *Complexity—The Emerging Science at the Edge of Order and Chaos* (New York: Touchstone/Simon and Schuster, 1992), p. 66.
2. *Riverside Dictionary*.
3. Margaret Wheatley and Myron Kellner-Rogers, *A Simpler Way*, audio literature, side 3 by arrangement with the original publisher (San Francisco, CA: Berrett-Koehler Publishers, 1996).
4. See Margaret Wheatley, *Leadership and the New Science—Learning about Organization from an Orderly Universe* (San Francisco: Berrett-Kohler Publishers, 1992); and Margaret Wheatley and Myron Kellner-Rogers, *A Simpler Way*; and work at Berkana Institute, Provo, Utah.
5. Wheatley and Kellner-Rogers, *A Simpler Way*, side 2.
6. "The New Millennium," an interview by Michael Thoms with Jean Houston from Palmer House Hilton at 1993 Parliament of the World's Religions, Chicago, Illinois, for New Dimensions Radio and Radio for Peace International, Program #2416, copyright New Dimensions Foundation, 1996.

Chapter 7: Performing the Magic

1. Gilley, *Leading from the Heart*, p. 208.
2. Ibid.
3. Brooke Warrick, "Changing American Values and the Effects on Business," keynote address at the 1996 International Conference on Spirituality in Business, November 10, 1996, Mazatlan, Mexico.

Chapter 8: Making It Happen

1. Tom Payne, *A Company of One—The Power of Independence in the Workplace* (Albuquerque, NM: Performance Press of Albuquerque, 1993).

Chapter 9: Could It Be Love?

1. Amanda McBroom, "The Rose" (Fox Fanfare Music, BMI).
2. Peck, *The Road Less Traveled*, p. 81.
3. Stephen R. Covey, *The Seven Habits of Highly Effective People: Powerful Lessons in Person Change* (New York: Fireside/Simon and Schuster, 1989) and *First Things First* (New York: Simon and Schuster, 1994).
4. Robert Fisher, *The Knight in Rusty Armor* (No. Hollywood, CA: Melvin Powers Wilshire Book Company, 1990), p. 69.
5. Ibid, p. 71.
6. Ibid.
7. Nelson Mandela, quoting Marianne Williamson in his 1994 Inaugural Address.

Chapter 11: The Power of Love

1. Hugh Downs, "Attitude," in Glen Van Ekerson, ed., *Speaker's Sourcebook II: Quotes, Stories, and Anecdotes for Every Occasion* (Prentice-Hall, 1994).

Butterworth-Heinemann Business Books . . . for Transforming Business

5th Generation Management: Co-creating Through Virtual Enterprising, Dynamic Teaming, and Knowledge Networking, Revised Edition
   Charles M. Savage, 0-7506-9701-6

After Atlantis: Working, Managing, and Leading in Turbulent Times
   Ned Hamson, 0-7506-9884-5

The Alchemy of Fear: How to Break the Corporate Trance and Create Your Company's Successful Future
   Kay Gilley, 0-7506-9909-4

Beyond Strategic Vision: Effective Corporate Action with Hoshin Planning
   Michael Cowley and Ellen Domb, 0-7506-9843-8

Beyond Time Management: Business with Purpose
   Robert A. Wright, 0-7506-9799-7

The Breakdown of Hierarchy: Communicating in the Evolving Workplace
   Eugene Marlow and Patricia O'Connor Wilson, 0-7056-9746-6

Business and the Feminine Principle: The Untapped Resource
   Carol R. Frenier, 0-7506-9829-2

Choosing the Future: The Power of Strategic Thinking
   Stuart Wells, 0-7506-9876-4

Cultivating Common Ground: Releasing the Power of Relationships at Work
   Daniel S. Hanson, 0-7506-9832-2

Flight of the Phoenix: Soaring to Success in the 21st Century
   John Whiteside and Sandra Egli, 0-7506-9798-9

Getting a Grip on Tomorrow: Your Guide to Survival and Success in the Changed World of Work
   Mike Johnson, 0-7506-9758-X

Innovation Strategy for the Knowledge Economy: The Ken Awakening
   Debra M. Amidon, 0-7506-9841-1

The Intelligence Advantage: Organizing for Complexity
   Michael D. McMaster, 0-7506-9792-X

Intuitive Imagery: A Resource at Work
John B. Pehrson and Susan E. Mehrtens, 0-7506-9805-5

The Knowledge Evolution: Expanding Organizational Intelligence
Verna Allee, 0-7506-9842-X

Leadership in a Challenging World: A Sacred Journey
Barbara Shipka, 0-7506-9750-4

Leading from the Heart: Choosing Courage over Fear in the Workplace
Kay Gilley, 0-7506-9835-7

Learning to Read the Signs: Reclaiming Pragmatism in Business
F. Byron Nahser, 0-7506-9901-9

Leveraging People and Profit: The Hard Work of Soft Management,
Bernard A. Nagle and Perry Pascarella, 0-7506-9961-2

Marketing Plans That Work: Targeting Growth and Profitability
Malcolm H.B. McDonald and Warren J. Keegan, 0-7506-9828-4

A Place to Shine: Emerging from the Shadows at Work
Daniel S. Hanson, 0-7506-9738-5

Power Partnering: A Strategy for Business Excellence in the 21st Century
Sean Gadman, 0-7506-9809-8

Putting Emotional Intelligence to Work: Successful Leadership is More Than IQ
David Ryback, 0-7506-9956-6

Resources for the Knowledge-Based Economy Series

The Knowledge Economy
Dale Neef, 0-7506-9936-1
Knowledge Management and Organizational Design
Paul S. Myers, 0-7506-9749-0
Knowledge Management Tool
Rudy L. Ruggles, III, 0-7506-9849-7
Knowledge in Organization
Laurence Prusak, 0-7506-9718-0
The Strategic Management of Intellectual Capital
David A. Klein, 0-7506-9850-0

Setting the PACE® in Product Development: A Guide to Product and Cycle-time Excellence
    Michael E. McGrath, 0-7506-9789-X

Time to Take Control: The Impact of Change on Corporate Computer Systems
    Tony Johnson, 0-7506-9863-2

The Transformation of Management
    Mike Davidson, 0-7506-9814-4

What is the Emperor Wearing? Truth-Telling in Business Relationships
    Laurie Weiss, 0-7506-9872-1

Who We Could Be at Work, Revised Edition
    Margaret A. Lulic, 0-7506-9739-3

Working From Your Core: Personal and Corporate Wisdom in a World of Change
    Sharon Seivert, 0-7506-9931-0

To purchase any Butterworth-Heinemann title, please visit your local bookstore or call 1-800-366-2665.

Leading from the Heart

Kay Gilley offers additional business wisdom in *Leading From the Heart: Choosing Courage Over Fear in the Workplace* (Butterworth-Heinemann, 1997).

Excerpt from the Introduction

This is a story of love, truth, courage, and growth for leaders and for organizations. It is a personal, sometimes deeply personal, story about my passion: guiding people and organizations to achieve their potential, working in community with one another. I fervently believe that people cannot achieve their full potential in an organization that is not achieving its own potential. By the same token, the organization cannot achieve its potential without the individuals within it achieving their own. None of us can hope to elicit from others qualities by which we ourselves are unwilling to live and work.

At the doorstep of the twenty-first century, organizations of all kinds—nonprofits, business, industry, and governments—face turbulence unlike any they have ever known. As chaos and confusion become more and more common and the pace of change accelerates dramatically, leaders must be able to work in conditions of increasing and continuing ambiguity: stable conditions simply don't exist any more. Leaders must display a deep, centered courage and authenticity that *en-courages* those around them to learn to deal with uncertainty, to keep the organization on course, and to be open to change. If organizations are to survive and thrive—indeed if our society is to survive and thrive—leaders must find new perspectives on leading.

A missing piece in most businesses has inhibited organizational unity—a phenomenon that holds people and organizations together, inspires them, and gives the resilience and responsiveness necessary to grow and develop in increasingly complex environments. This missing component isn't linear, logical, rational, or even explainable: it just happens when the "magicians"—the leaders—create the right conditions. Then, although the workplace experience may swing from exciting to peaceful and satisfying, people feel happy and energized. This "magic" generates the capacity to do the seemingly undoable.

Many traditional, hierarchical organizations have failed or faltered in the past two decades. Others hope for the easy, quick fix and hang on through a desperate and accelerating cycle of organizational change efforts. Although efforts at workplace democracy, employee involvement, and high performance work systems generally improve results and increase satisfaction, they often leave the people in them feeling overworked and burned out. Leaders at all levels of all organizations must reevaluate their perspectives on work and begin to find ways to work which energize and renew the people within them.

Joe is a client of mine. He is fifty, and his current company is the largest of several largely successful ventures he has started during his career. Joe's present company is very promising. Applying innovative approaches to standard ways of delivering his service, he has developed a model that is drawing industry recognition and investment interest nationally. His other ventures were "small potatoes" compared to this company's potential, and the work I have done with him has helped him identify his fears about moving forward. He is now committed to building the company to its potential.

Some time ago I attended a meeting in which Joe talked to a group of his managers about the future of his young and rapidly growing company. He shares his hopes and dreams, and he shares his fears about continuing to grow the company. Even as his voice breaks and a tear comes to his eye, he shares with the managers both his sense of responsibility to the employees and the company's clients and his faith that the team that helped bring the company this far will continue to keep it healthy and prosperous. He asks for their commitment to take the company to its full potential. There is great enthusiasm: as one manager later put it, "I'm really jazzed to make this happen!" And the growth is happening.

In the same city just a few miles away, Ted, the leader of a similar organization gives a similar speech, but Ted lacks the courage to name and address his fears. He tries to make all the managers happy by telling them what he thinks they want to hear, but this approach makes the managers question his integrity. His past exaggerations have led to skepticism and cynicism among his employees. People listen dutifully as Ted fidgets and then recites his remarks despite his feelings of unease. When he is finished, his audience asks itself one question: "Will it *really* happen?" Then, a manager asks whether they have to go back to work; after all, it is 3:30 p.m. on Friday. Ted, feeling let down, goes back to his office.

Why is this "magic" present in some organizations and not in others? In this book I discuss the nonquantifiable, intangible aspects of organizations that can emanate from the leadership at all levels to produce this magic and explain what allows Joe to accomplish incredible growth with dynamic flexibility while Ted and his company trudge along and just survive from one day to the other.

I would not have been open to reading, much less writing, this book just a few years ago, when I thought that any worthwhile concepts should be reducible to a set of defined parameters and cause-effect actions. Many readers of this book may share the same opinion. I ask those readers to have faith, while I acknowledge that I once would not have mustered such faith myself.

Although I have written extensively over the years, in the early stages of this project I spent several days wrestling with words in a new way. After the words began to flow, the solution to a puzzle which I had been seeking for four years began unfolding on the computer screen. This experience reminded me of a line from Meg Wheatley's book *Leadership and the New Science*: "Disorder can play a critical role in giving birth to new, higher forms of order." Earlier I had looked for surface order and had looked at *things*, at what people were *doing*: behaviors, practices, approaches, training. The solution to my puzzle, however, was not to be found in *doing*. The answer was in a higher form of order.

We must look at the ways we run organizations as we approach the twenty-first century. We must stop focusing on what we *do* and begin to consider who we *are* as human beings in community with each other. The doing and the being in our organizations are both important for accomplishing our purposes, but we must balance our focus in the workplace. In this book I emphasize *being*, because traditionally we have only been concerned with the *doing*.

When we experience people as machines or as stagnant entities, we experience organizations in the same way. Neither we nor our organizations are mechanistic or static. Organizations are living systems of human beings. The intangible missing pieces that machine models lack are the very things living systems have: joy and vitality, which work can and should bring to people.

Ignoring the personal integrity that people bring to their work and how they have been in relationship to that work can cause *doing* to fail partly or completely. Leaders wrongly expect *doing* to equal *results*.

What we do = Results we get

Instead the invisible factor of *who we are* is integral to the results.

What we do + Who we are = Results we get

Our quantitative minds have tried and tried to retain equilibrium while ignoring the critical *who we are* component. When we take *who we are* out of one side of the equation, forces bent on equilibrium subtract it from the results. Yet we fail to understand why the results we get never seem to be what we expect, at least not over the long term.

What we do = Results we get (who we are)

We always seem to get something less than the results we expect or hope we will get. As managers tinker and tinker with *what we do*, the failure to acknowledge the *who we are* factor creates greater and greater disequilibrium, weakness, awkwardness, and the inability to flex and change on a dime as conditions require. Tinkering with what we do can produce moderate improvements and even significant short-term improvements; but tinkering burns people out and leaves them sapped of creativity in the workplace and sapped of energy for the rest of life. By itself, changing what we do hasn't produced the results we want over the long run, and it never will until who we are is taken into account.

Excerpt from Chapter 1: Accepting Our Silent Earthquakes

In the winter of 1989–1990, the world began to change. A slow, silent earthquake began to crumble physical structures as great as the Berlin Wall and symbolic structures of monolithic bureaucracy like the statue of Lenin in Red Square. The new leaders included poets and playwrights who had struggled to keep the spirits of whole nations of people alive amid systems that sought to stifle the individual spirit. After generations of struggle for survival within confining structures, millions were "liberated" into a life of chaos. They had broken from the yoke of totalitarianism without having any structure or order to put in its place. They found themselves in the midst of the pain, confusion, and struggle that chaos inevitably brings. Chaos is a creative incubator from which a higher order can emerge, but chaos can be frightening. It can be frightening for the people plunged into the midst of it, for those charged to lead them, and for those who watch and wait and feel powerless to help. Fear can breed protective measures, violence aimed at ensuring the survival of one's own family, friends, and kind. At its extreme, fear can breed genocide.

Many of those propelled into the chaos are angry. Some expected a painless metamorphosis—new birth without the gestation period or the pains of labor. Others feel angry and victimized because they didn't choose this quiet revolution. Who will take care of them now? Still others are angry because quiet revolution hasn't been so quiet after all. They feel cheated because nations they believed would protect them did little but watch the decay, the war, and the genocide. The people who started the earthquake instinctively knew that there had to be a better way to live—a life in which they could not only survive but could thrive. They cleared the way to make it happen. Yet generations of programming left their native instincts about how to live in a different way anesthetized.

Anyone who has gone through any of life's transitions probably recognizes the signs. The large-scale social transition in Eastern Europe was not unlike the death of a parent or spouse, a divorce, the birth of a child, or a midlife crisis. In each there is the possibility for a better life, and in each there is a sense of loss. In each there are anger, fear, and often guilt and resentment. In each, when times are rough, there is wishing, maybe even trying, to go back, yet people know that it would never work. In each there is a chaotic time of gathering courage, patience, faith, and the commitment to move forward; a period of reassessment, exploration, discovery, and decisions about where life will lead us. To survive any of these personal transitions and thrive, we need a clear sense of direction, strong values, and a belief in our own ability to weather the storm and to have a better life because of our experience.

An Invisible Earthquake at Home

The slow, silent earthquake of Eastern Europe is not unlike the silent, invisible earthquake occurring in our U. S. workplaces. I often hear employers lament, "People just don't care anymore" or "You just can't get good help." Their complaints may vary. They talk about halfhearted performance. They deplore that employees don't think about what they're doing. They bemoan lack of commitment and "punching the clock" attitudes. They mourn a "lack of respect." They anguish about how careful and guarded they must be and how laws have tied their hands. And when the finger of blame is pointed, they blame everyone. The state and federal governments are blamed for excessive legislation and regulation; then they are blamed for not doing something. Managers, employees, schools, and parents are blamed for ineptness or indifference. International competition is blamed. Labor unions are blamed. The blame goes on and on.

At the same time, employees who have grown accustomed to secure employment if they "just do their jobs" have been thrust into roles that force them to give more of themselves—their creativity, teamwork, and problem-solving skills. Others downsized out of midmanagement jobs after many years are disillusioned because "After all those years, this is what I get!" People know instinctively that there has to be a better way. Yet the better way is not readily apparent. New management models have toyed with different forms, but little has really changed.

What is it that the employers want? They want energetic employees. They want enthusiasm, excitement, and initiative. They want employees who love their work—who put their heart into what they are doing. They want employees who care about the company, who see that everyone has to work together for the company to succeed. They want commitment and a spirited work force. They want trust. They want love. The employers want from employees what they often unknowingly are unable or unwilling to give: *themselves*. Employers have been unwilling or unable to give the people that work for them the benefit of the doubt, the trust, the faith, the risk taking and the commitment that they want and expect workers to give them.

Kay Gilley is CEO and senior consultant of Intentional Leadership Systems, a firm dedicated to building conscious leaders and intentional organizations. Bringing over thirty-two years' experience to her work, this seasoned manager is dedicated to healing the separation with self that has limited individuals in achieving their potential in organizations. In her public speaking and her work with individual leaders and intact leadership teams, she breaks her clients' individual and corporate trances so that organizations can rediscover life, foster latent creativity, and reclaim their whole potential.

Ms. Gilley is author of two books and coauthor of a third. *Leading from the Heart: Choosing Courage over Fear in the Workplace* is designed to assist leaders at all organizational levels to learn how to be fully present and conscious in their work and in their lives. It encourages individuals to choose a conscious path and assists them in discovering how to accomplish that goal. *The Alchemy of Fear: How to Break the Corporate Trance and Create Your Company's Successful Future* transforms fear into teacher, friend, and guide to success. Ms. Gilley is currently working on a new book about conscious leaders and intentional organizations. She is also coauthor of *The New Bottom Line: Bringing Heart and Soul to Business*.

The author may be contacted at the following address:

c/o Intentional Leadership Systems
505 Woodwinds Drive
Durham, NC 27713
(919) 493-5633